Nelson Comprehension

Teacher's Book 1
for Books 1 & 2

CONTENTS

How Nelson Comprehension Works	2
The National Curriculum in England	6
Scotland Curriculum for Excellence	8
Curriculum for Wales	10
The Curriculum in Northern Ireland	13
The Cambridge International Primary Curriculum	14
Book 1	16
Book 2	38
Key Stage 1 Example Test Paper Answers	60

OXFORD
UNIVERSITY PRESS

How Nelson Comprehension Works

YEAR	PUPIL BOOK	RESOURCES & ASSESSMENT	REVISION BOOK	TEACHING SUPPORT
YEAR 1 / P2	Pupil Book 1	Resources and Assessment Book For Books 1 & 2		Teacher's Book 1
YEAR 2 / P3	Pupil Book 2			
YEAR 3 / P4	Pupil Book 3	Resources and Assessment Book For Books 3 & 4		Teacher's Book 2
YEAR 4 / P5	Pupil Book 4			
YEAR 5 / P6	Pupil Book 5	Resources and Assessment Book For Books 5 & 6		
YEAR 6 / P7	Pupil Book 6		Revision Book	

Nelson Comprehension is an easy-to-use, rigorous programme for the teaching and practising of comprehension skills for children aged 5 – 11. It covers all types of comprehension — from literal understanding to higher-order skills such as inference, deduction and using prior knowledge or personal experience to help understand a text.

Each **Pupil Book** contains ten units. At key stage 1, each unit comprises two sets of texts and questions; at key stage 2, each unit comprises three sets of texts and questions. The texts and questions in each unit share the same genre and learning focus: for example, fiction extracts that focus on characters' feelings.

Questions are differentiated through their colour-coding, so you can choose which sets of questions you want the children to tackle, depending on which skills they need to practise.

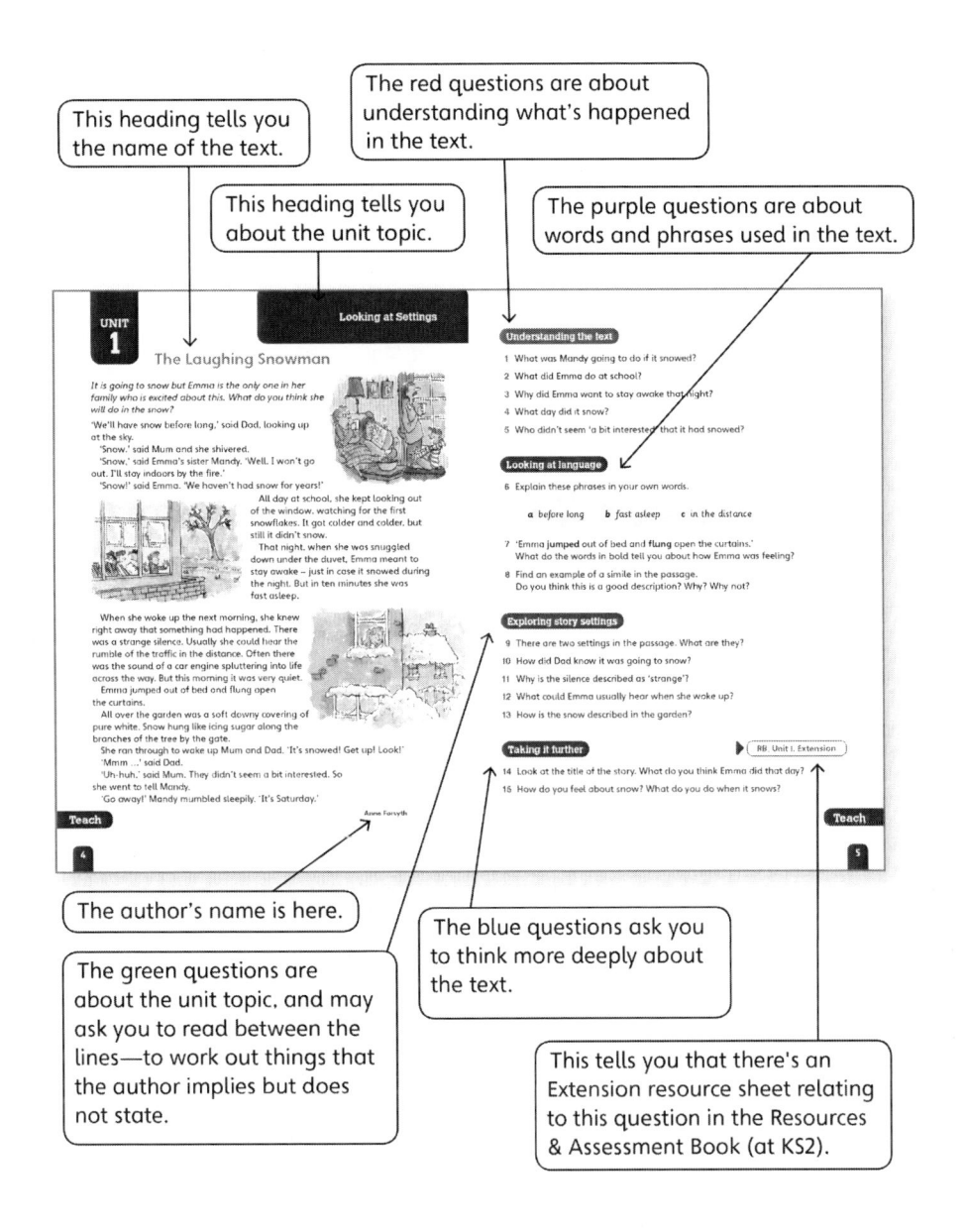

- This heading tells you the name of the text.
- The red questions are about understanding what's happened in the text.
- This heading tells you about the unit topic.
- The purple questions are about words and phrases used in the text.
- The author's name is here.
- The green questions are about the unit topic, and may ask you to read between the lines—to work out things that the author implies but does not state.
- The blue questions ask you to think more deeply about the text.
- This tells you that there's an Extension resource sheet relating to this question in the Resources & Assessment Book (at KS2).

Using a dictionary
Purple vocabulary questions will often ask children to look up the meaning of words in a dictionary. At key stage 2, children may not find these words in a junior dictionary and may need to consult an accessible full dictionary, such as www.oxforddictionaries.com.

There are three **Resources and Assessment Books**: one for Pupil Books 1 & 2, one for Pupil Books 3 & 4 and one for Pupil Books 5 & 6. Two differentiated, photocopiable resource sheets are given for every text in the Pupil Books, offering further practice of comprehension skills.

The **Support** sheet offers more practice of literal comprehension skills.

The **Extension** sheet provides questions and activities for those ready to be challenged further. At key stage 2, some of the final Extension resource sheets in a unit will ask children to think about all three texts in the unit.

The **Teacher's Book** guides you through each unit, providing:

- a quick-reference spread from the Pupil Book.
- suggestions for discussion.
- answers to the
  - Pupil Book questions.
  - Support resource sheets from the Resources and Assessment Books.
  - Example test papers for Years 2 and 4 (P3 and 5) from the Resources and Assessment Books.
  - Example test papers for Year 6 from the Revision Book.
- answers have not been provided for the Extension resource sheets as these require individual responses from the children.

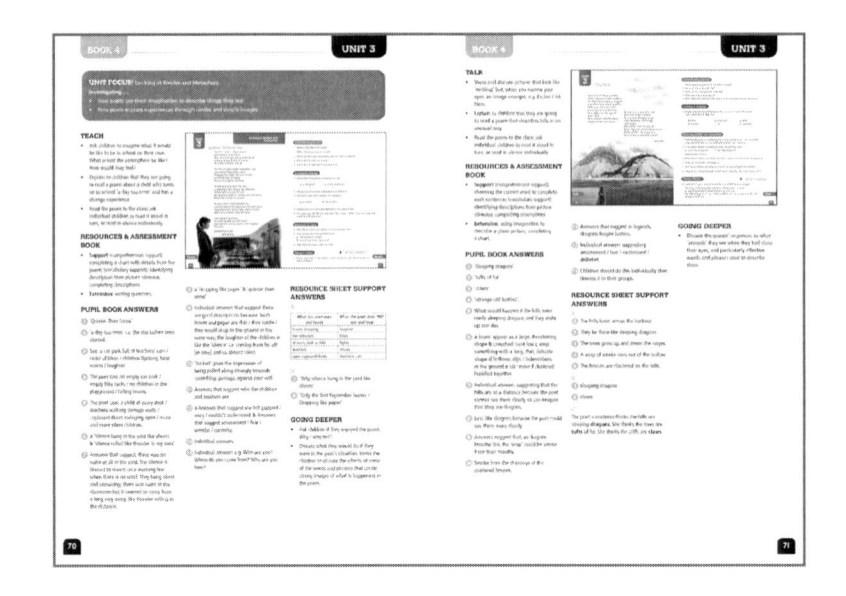

The **Revision Book** contains three end-of-key stage 2 example test papers.

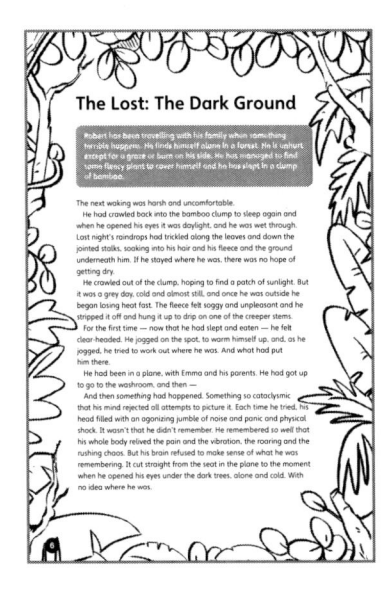

Assessment

Resources and Assessment Book for Books 1 & 2 contains two photocopiable end of key stage 1 example reading test papers, so that you can prepare children for their Year 2 reading test.

Paper 1 consists of a combined reading prompt and answer booklet. You will need to spend at least five minutes introducing the paper, reading the practice text, and modelling the practice questions with the whole class. Children will then have 30 minutes (not strictly timed) to read the text and answer the questions in the paper.

Paper 2 consists of a reading booklet containing one fiction and one non-fiction text, and a question booklet. Children have 40 minutes to read the texts and answer the questions in this paper.

More information on how to administer these tests can be found in the *Resources and Assessment Book for Books 1 & 2*.

At key stage 2 *Resources and Assessment Book for Books 3 & 4* contains two example reading test papers for Year 4 children, enabling you to monitor children's progress and help avoid a plateauing in their progression. The two Year 4 papers each consist of a reading booklet, containing one fiction and one non-fiction text, and a question booklet. Children should be given one hour (not strictly timed) to read the texts in the booklet and answer the questions.

The *Revision Book* contains three end of key stage 2 example test papers, enabling you to prepare your Year 6 children for their reading test, and give them confidence as they enter the test. Each test comprises a reading booklet, containing one fiction text, one non-fiction text and one poem; and a question and answer booklet. Children should be given one hour to read the three texts in the reading booklet and complete the questions at their own pace. They should be encouraged to read one text at a time and then answer the questions on that text, before moving on to the next text.

Teaching approaches

Flexible teaching

Nelson Comprehension has been written so that any set of text and questions in the Pupil Books can be used for whole-class teaching, group work, or individual written work.

Teach Talk Write

If you choose, you can follow the *Teach Talk Write* approach for *Nelson Comprehension*, which enables you to work through each unit first as a class or in groups and then individually.

At Key Stage 1

The first text and questions in each unit is **Teach / Talk**: you can read the extract to the children and then answer the questions as a whole class or in groups, discussing the text, modelling key comprehension skills and demonstrating to children how they can find answers to the questions.

The second text and questions in each unit is **Write**: children can try reading the text and answering the questions on their own.

At Key Stage 2

The first text and questions in each unit is **Teach**: you can read the text to the class, and then work through the questions together, modelling comprehension skills and showing children how to find answers to the questions.

The second text and questions in each unit is **Talk**: children can read the text in turn and then attempt the questions in groups.

The third text and questions in each unit is **Write**: children read the text and answer the text individually.

The National Curriculum in England

Nelson Comprehension provides a carefully structured course for teaching comprehension skills to children in Years 1 – 6. The course is designed to build children's competence and confidence in reading comprehension, while providing lively, engaging extracts which they will enjoy. The chart below matches units in the Pupil Books to the National Curriculum in England. The Scope and Sequence charts for each book give a detailed breakdown of the comprehension skills covered in the Resources and Assessment Books as well as the Pupil Books.

Programme of Study	Book 1	Book 2	Book 3	Book 4	Book 5	Book 6
YEAR 1						
Pupils should be taught to:						
develop pleasure in reading, motivation to read, vocabulary and understanding by:						
listening to and discussing a wide range of poems, stories and non-fiction at a level beyond that at which they can read independently	Units 2, 3, 4, 5, 6, 7, 8, 9	Units 1, 6	Unit 7	Units 2, 4, 10	Units 3, 5, 10	Units 8, 9, 10
being encouraged to link what they read or hear to their own experiences	Units 1, 5, 7, 9, 10	Units 1, 2, 9, 10	Units 1, 6, 8	Units 3, 4	Unit 4	Units 3, 4, 9
becoming very familiar with key stories, fairy stories and traditional tales, retelling them and considering their particular characteristics	Units 3, 6	Unit 3	Unit 5	Unit 8	Units 1, 9, 10	Units 2, 8
recognising and joining in with predictable phrases	Units 3, 5, 10	Units 5, 10				
learning to appreciate rhymes and poems, and to recite some by heart	Units 5, 10	Units 5, 10	Unit 3	Unit 3	Unit 6	Units 4, 9
discussing word meanings, linking new meanings to those already known	Units 3, 5, 6, 7, 8, 9	Units 1, 3, 4, 6, 7	All units	All units	All units	All units
understand both the books they can already read accurately and fluently and those they listen to by:						
drawing on what they already know or on background information and vocabulary provided by the teacher	Units 1, 2, 4, 5, 6, 8, 9	Units 1, 2, 9, 10	All units	All units	All units	All units
checking that the text makes sense to them as they read, and correcting inaccurate reading	All units	All units	All units	All units	All units	All units
discussing the significance of the title and events	Units 1, 5	Unit 2	Units 1, 2, 9	Units 3, 4, 7	Unit 8	
making inferences on the basis of what is being said and done	Units 1, 2, 3, 4, 5, 6, 7, 10	Units 1, 3, 7, 9, 10	Units 1, 3, 5, 7, 8, 10	Units 1, 2, 3, 5, 7, 8, 9, 10	Units 1, 2, 3, 6, 7, 8, 9, 10	Units 1, 2, 4, 5, 6, 7, 8, 9
predicting what might happen on the basis of what has been read so far	Units 1, 3, 6, 8	Units 1, 3	Units 1, 5, 7, 10	Units 1, 8, 9, 10	Units 1, 7, 9, 10	Units 2, 6
participate in discussion about what is read to them, taking turns and listening to what others say	All units	All units	All units	All units	All units	All units
explain clearly their understanding of what is read to them	All units	All units	All units	All units	All units	All units
YEAR 2						
Pupils should be taught to:						
develop pleasure in reading, motivation to read, vocabulary and understanding by:						
listening to, discussing and expressing views about a wide range of contemporary and classic poetry, stories and non-fiction at a level beyond that at which they can read independently	Units 2, 3, 4, 5, 6, 7, 8, 9	Units 1, 6	Unit 7	Units 2, 4, 10	Units 3, 5, 10	Units 8, 9, 10

The National Curriculum in England (cont.)

Programme of Study	Book 1	Book 2	Book 3	Book 4	Book 5	Book 6
discussing the sequence of events in books and how items of information are related	Units 1, 4, 7, 9	Unit 2				Units 1, 5
becoming increasingly familiar with and retelling a wider range of stories, fairy stories and traditional tales	Units 3, 6, 8	Unit 3	Unit 5	Units 1, 5, 7, 10	Units 1, 9, 10	Units 2, 8
being introduced to non-fiction books that are structured in different ways	Units 2, 4, 9	Units 2, 4, 7, 9	Units 2, 4, 6, 8, 9	Units 2, 4, 6	Units 2, 4, 5, 8	Units 1, 3, 5, 7, 10
recognising simple recurring literary language in stories and poetry	Units 3, 5, 10	Units 5, 10				
discussing and clarifying the meanings of words, linking new meanings to known vocabulary	Units 3, 5, 6, 7, 8, 9	Units 1, 3, 4, 6, 7	All units	All units	All units	All units
discussing their favourite words and phrases		Unit 10				Units 4, 9
continuing to build up a repertoire of poems learnt by heart, appreciating these and reciting some, with appropriate intonation to make the meaning clear			Unit 3			
understand both the books that they can already read accurately and fluently and those that they listen to by:						
drawing on what they already know or on background information and vocabulary provided by the teacher	Units 1, 6, 7, 8, 9	Units 1, 2, 9, 10	All units	All units	All units	All units
checking that the text makes sense to them as they read, and correcting inaccurate reading	All units	All units	All units	All units	All units	All units
making inferences on the basis of what is being said and done	Units 1, 2, 3, 4, 5, 6, 7, 10	Units 1, 3, 7, 9, 10	Units 1, 3, 5, 7, 8, 10	Units 1, 2, 3, 5, 7, 8, 9, 10	Units 1, 2, 3, 6, 7, 8, 9, 10	Units 1, 2, 4, 5, 6, 7, 8, 9
answering and asking questions	All units	All units	All units	All units	All units	All units
predicting what might happen on the basis of what has been read so far	Units 1, 3, 6, 8	Units 1, 3	Units 1, 5, 7, 10	Units 1, 8, 9, 10	Units 1, 7, 9, 10	Units 2, 6
participate in discussion about books, poems and other works that are read to them and those that they can read for themselves, taking turns and listening to what others say	All units	All units	All units	All units	All units	All units
explain and discuss their understanding of books, poems and other material, both those that they listen to and those that they read for themselves	All units	All units	All units	All units	All units	All units

Scotland Curriculum for Excellence: literacy experiences and outcomes

	Book 1	Book 2	Book 3	Book 4	Book 5	Book 6
YEAR 1						
I regularly select and read, listen to or watch texts which I enjoy and find interesting, and I can explain why I prefer certain texts and authors. (LIT 1-11a / LIT 2-11a)	Units 2, 3, 4, 5, 6, 7, 8, 9, 10	Units 1, 3, 5, 6, 10	Units 3, 5, 7	Units 2, 3, 4, 8, 10	Units 1, 3, 5, 6, 9, 10	Units 2, 4, 8, 9, 10
I can use my knowledge of sight vocabulary, phonics, context clues, punctuation and grammar to read with understanding and expression. (ENG 1-12a)	All units	All units	All units	All units	All units	All units
I am learning to select and use strategies and resources before I read, and as I read, to help make the meaning of texts clear. (LIT 1-13a)	All units	All units	All units	All units	All units	All units
Using what I know about the features of different types of texts, I can find, select, sort and use information for a specific purpose. (LIT 1-14a)	Units 1, 2, 4, 5, 6, 8, 9	Units 1, 2, 9, 10	All units	All units	All units	All units
I am learning to make notes under given headings and use them to understand information, explore ideas and problems and create new texts. (LIT 1-15a)						
To show my understanding across different areas of learning, I can identify and consider the purpose and main ideas of a text. (LIT 1-16a)	Units 1, 5	Unit 2	Units 1, 2, 9	Units 3, 4, 7	Unit 8	
To show my understanding, I can respond to different kinds of questions and other close reading tasks and I am learning to create some questions of my own. (ENG 1-17a)	All units	All units	All units	All units	All units	All units
To help me develop an informed view, I can recognize the difference between fact and opinion. (LIT 1-18a)				Unit 2	Unit 8	Units 7, 10
I can share my thoughts about structure, characters and/or setting, recognize the writer's message and relate it to my own experiences, and comment on the effective choice of words and other features. (ENG 1-19a)	All units	All units	All units	All units	All units	All units
YEAR 2						
I regularly select and read, listen to or watch texts which I enjoy and find interesting, and I can explain why I prefer certain texts and authors. (LIT 1-11a / LIT 2-11a)	Units 2, 3, 4, 5, 6, 7, 8, 9	Units 1, 6	Unit 7	Units 2, 4, 10	Units 3, 5, 10	Units 8, 9, 10
I can use my knowledge of sight vocabulary, phonics, context clues, punctuation and grammar to read with understanding and expression. (ENG 1-12a)	All units	All units	All units	All units	All units	All units
I am learning to select and use strategies and resources before I read, and as I read, to help make the meaning of texts clear. (LIT 1-13a)	Units 1, 3, 5, 6, 7, 8, 9	Units 1, 2, 3, 4, 6, 7, 9, 10	All units	All units	All units	All units
Using what I know about the features of different types of texts, I can find, select, sort and use information for a specific purpose. (LIT 1-14a)	Units 2, 4, 9	Units 2, 4, 7, 9	Units 2, 4, 6, 8, 9	Units 2, 4, 6	Units 2, 4, 5, 8	Units 1, 3, 5, 7, 10
I am learning to make notes under given headings and use them to understand information, explore ideas and problems and create new texts. (LIT 1-15a)						
To show my understanding across different areas of learning, I can identify and consider the purpose and main ideas of a text. (LIT 1-16a)	All units	All units	All units	All units	All units	All units

Scotland Curriculum (cont.)

	Book 1	Book 2	Book 3	Book 4	Book 5	Book 6
To show my understanding, I can respond to different kinds of questions and other close reading tasks and I am learning to create some questions of my own. (ENG 1-17a)	All units	All units	All units	All units	All units	All units
To help me develop an informed view, I can recognize the difference between fact and opinion. (LIT 1-18a)				Unit 2	Unit 8	Units 7, 10
I can share my thoughts about structure, characters and/or setting, recognize the writer's message and relate it to my own experiences, and comment on the effective choice of words and other features. (ENG 1-19a)	All units	All units	All units	All units	All units	All units

Curriculum for Wales

Programme of Study for English: Reading

YEAR 1

Reading: Strategies

	Book 1	Book 2	Book 3	Book 4	Book 5	Book 6
choose reading materials and explain what the text is about and why they like it (Y1_ReadStrat.1)	Units 5, 10	Units 5, 10	Unit 3	Unit 3	Unit 6	Units 4, 9
talk about features of books such as contents page and titles (Y1_ReadStrat.2)	All units	All units	All units	All units	All units	All units
link and identify spoken sounds to blends of letters and letter names (Y1_ReadStrat.3)						
recognize and use an increasing number of phonemes and their corresponding graphemes when blending and segmenting words of up to two syllables (Y1_ReadStrat.4)						
apply the following reading strategies with increasing independence – phonic strategies to decode words (Y1_ReadStrat.5i)						
– recognition of high-frequency words (Y1_ReadStrat.5ii)						
– context clues, e.g. prior knowledge (Y1_ReadStrat.5iii)	Units 1, 2, 4, 5, 6, 8, 9	Units 1, 2, 9, 10	All units	All units	All units	All units
– graphic and syntactic clues (Y1_ReadStrat.5iv)						
– self-correction, including re-reading and reading ahead (Y1_ReadStrat.5v)	All units	All units	All units	All units	All units	All units
track print with eyes, finger pointing only at points of difficulty (Y1_ReadStrat.6)						
decode unknown words containing blended consonants and vowels by using strategies, e.g. segmenting phonemes, onset and rime (Y1_ReadStrat.7)						
read suitable texts with accuracy and fluency (Y1_ReadStrat.8)	All units	All units	All units	All units	All units	All units
read aloud with attention to full stops and question marks (Y1_ReadStrat.9)	All units	All units	All units	All units	All units	All units
read aloud with expression, showing awareness of exclamation and speech marks (Y1_ReadStrat.10)	All units	All units	All units	All units	All units	All units
identify simple text features such as titles and pictures to indicate what the text is about (Y1_ReadStrat.11)	Units 1, 5	Unit 2	Units 1, 2, 9	Units 3, 4, 7	Unit 8	
look for clues in the text to understand information (Y1_ReadStrat.12)	Units 1, 2, 3, 4, 5, 6, 7, 8, 10	Units 1, 3, 7, 9, 10	Units 1, 3, 5, 7, 8, 10	Units 1, 2, 3, 5, 7, 8, 9, 10	Units 1, 2, 3, 6, 7, 8, 9, 10	Units 1, 2, 4, 5, 6, 7, 8, 9
understand the meaning of visual features and link to written text, e.g. illustrations, photographs, diagrams and charts (Y1_ReadStrat.13)	Units 2, 4, 9	Units 2, 4, 7, 9	Units 2, 4, 6, 8, 9	Units 2, 4, 6	Units 2, 4, 5, 8	Units 1, 3, 5, 7, 10
identify words and pictures on-screen which are related to a topic (Y1_ReadStrat.14)						

Reading: Comprehension

	Book 1	Book 2	Book 3	Book 4	Book 5	Book 6
retell events from a narrative in the right order (Y1_ReadComp.1)	Units 3, 6	Unit 3	Unit 5	Unit 8	Units 1, 9, 10	Units 2, 8
identify information related to the subject of a text (Y1_ReadComp.2)	All units	All units	All units	All units	All units	All units

Curriculum for Wales (cont.)

	Book 1	Book 2	Book 3	Book 4	Book 5	Book 6
recall details from information texts (Y1_ReadComp.3)	All units	All units	All units	All units	All units	All units
use personal experience to support understanding of texts (Y1_ReadComp.4)	Units 1, 5, 7, 9, 10	Units 1, 2, 9, 10	Units 1, 6, 8	Units 3, 4	Unit 4	Units 3, 4, 9
use prediction in stories, adding more detail (Y1_ReadComp.5)	Units 1, 3, 6, 8	Units 1, 3	Units 1, 5, 7, 10	Units 1, 8, 9, 10	Units 1, 7, 9, 10	Units 2, 6
Reading: Response and Analysis						
express a view about the information in a text (Y1_ReadResp.1)	All units	All units	All units	All units	All units	All units
explore language, information and events in texts (Y1_ReadResp.2)	All units	All units	All units	All units	All units	All units
make links between texts read and other information about the topic (Y1_ReadResp.3)	Units 1, 2, 4, 5, 6, 8, 9	Units 1, 2, 9, 10	All units	All units	All units	All units
YEAR 2						
Reading: Strategies						
choose reading materials independently, giving reasons for their choices (Y2_ReadStrat.1)	Units 2, 3, 4, 5, 6, 7, 8, 9	Units 1, 6	Unit 7	Units 2, 4, 10	Units 3, 5, 10	Units 8, 9, 10
use contents page and glossary within a range of texts (Y2_ReadStrat.2)			Unit 2			
confidently use all phonemes and their corresponding graphemes when blending and segmenting polysyllabic words (Y2_ReadStrat.3)						
apply the following reading strategies with increasing independence to a range of familiar and unfamiliar texts: – phonic strategies (Y2_ReadStrat.4i)						
– recognition of high-frequency words (Y2_ReadStrat.4ii)						
– context clues, e.g. prior knowledge (Y2_ReadStrat.4iii)						
– graphic and syntactic clues (Y2_ReadStrat.4 iv)						
self-correction (Y2_ReadStrat.4v)						
track a page of print with eyes without difficulty (Y2_ReadStrat.5)	All units	All units	All units	All units	All units	All units
decode text with unfamiliar content or vocabulary sustaining comprehension throughout (Y2_ReadStrat.6)	All units	All units	All units	All units	All units	All units
read a range of suitable texts with increasing accuracy and fluency (Y2_ReadStrat.7)	Units 2, 3, 4, 5, 6, 7, 8, 9	Units 1, 6	Unit 7	Units 2, 4, 10	Units 3, 5, 10	Units 8, 9, 10
read aloud with attention to punctuation, including full stops, question, exclamation and speech marks, varying intonation and pace (Y2_ReadStrat.4)	All units	All units	All units	All units	All units	All units
identify and use text features, e.g. Titles, headings and pictures, to locate and understand specific information (Y2_ReadStrat.5)	Units 2, 4, 9	Units 2, 4, 7, 9	Units 2, 4, 6, 8, 9	Units 2, 4, 6	Units 2, 4, 5, 8	Units 1, 3, 5, 7, 10
look for key words to find out what the text is about (Y2_ReadStrat.6)	All units	All units	All units	All units	All units	All units
use the different features of texts to make meaning, e.g. pictures, charts, and layout (Y2_ReadStrat.7)	Units 2, 4, 9	Units 2, 4, 7, 9	Units 2, 4, 6, 8, 9	Units 2, 4, 6	Units 2, 4, 5, 8	Units 1, 3, 5, 7, 10

Curriculum for Wales (cont.)

	Book 1	Book 2	Book 3	Book 4	Book 5	Book 6
identify key words to search for information on-screen, and modify search words as necessary (Y2_ReadStrat.8)						
Reading: Comprehension						
recall and retell narratives and information from texts with some details (Y2_ReadComp.1)	Units 3, 6, 8	Unit 3	Unit 5	Units 1, 5, 7, 10	Units 1, 9, 10	Units 2, 8
identify information from a text accurately and sort into categories or headings (Y2_ReadComp.2)						
explain relevant details from texts (Y2_ReadComp.3)	Units 2, 4, 9	Units 2, 4, 7, 9	Units 2, 4, 6, 8, 9	Units 2, 4, 6	Units 2, 4, 5, 8	Units 1, 3, 5, 7, 10
draw upon relevant personal experience and prior knowledge to support understanding of texts (Y2_ReadComp.4)	Units 1, 3, 5, 6, 7, 8, 9	Units 1, 2, 3, 4, 6, 7, 9, 10	All units	All units	All units	All units
refine and revise predictions in fiction and non-fiction texts (Y2_ReadComp.5)	Units 1, 3, 6, 8	Units 1, 3	Units 1, 5, 7, 10	Units 1, 8, 9, 10	Units 1, 7, 9, 10	Units 2, 6
Reading: Response and Analysis						
express views about information and details in a text, considering content, ideas, presentation, organization and the language used (Y2_ReadResp.1)	Units 1, 2, 3, 4, 5, 6, 7, 8, 9, 10	Units 1, 3, 6, 7, 9, 10	Units 1, 3, 5, 7, 8, 10	Units 1, 2, 3, 4, 5, 7, 8, 9, 10	Units 1, 2, 3, 5, 6, 7, 8, 9, 10	Units 1, 2, 4, 5, 6, 7, 8, 9, 10
show understanding and express opinions about language, information and events in texts (Y2_ReadResp.2)	Units 1, 3, 4, 5, 7, 9, 10	Units 2, 5, 10				Units 1, 5
make links between texts read and new information about the topic (Y2_ReadResp.3)	Units 1, 6, 7, 8, 9	Units 1, 2, 9, 10	Units 2, 4, 6, 8, 9	Units 2, 4, 6	Units 2, 4, 5, 8	Units 1, 3, 5, 7, 10

Northern Ireland

Levels of Progression in Communication across the curriculum

	Book 1	Book 2	Book 3	Book 4	Book 5	Book 6
YEAR 1						
Level 1						
show understanding of the meaning carried by print, pictures and images (L1_com_read.1)	All units	All units	All units	All units	All units	All units
understand that words are made up of sounds and syllables and that sounds are represented by letters (L1_com_read.2i)						
use reading strategies (L1_com_read.2ii)	All units	All units	All units	All units	All units	All units
read and understand familiar words, signs and symbols in the environment (L1_com_read.3i)	All units	Units 1, 2, 3, 4, 5, 6, 7, 9, 10	All units	All units	All units	All units
use visual clues to locate information (L1_com_read.3ii)	Units 1, 2, 3, 4, 5, 6, 7, 10	Units 1, 3, 7, 9, 10	All units	All units	All units	All units
use language associated with texts (L1_com_read.4)						
talk about what they read and answer questions (L1_com_read.5)	All units	All units	All units	All units	All units	All units
Level 2						
understand, recount and sequence events and information (L2_com_read.1)	Units 1, 4, 7, 9	Unit 2				Units 1, 5
use a range of reading strategies (L2_com_read.2)	All units	All units	All units	All units	All units	All units
select information for a purpose (L2_com_read.3i)	Units 2, 4, 9	Units 2, 4, 7, 9	Units 2, 4, 6, 8, 9	Units 2, 4, 6	Units 2, 4, 5, 8	Units 1, 3, 5, 7, 10
use basic alphabetical knowledge and visual clues to locate information (L2_com_read.3ii)	Units 1, 2, 3, 4, 5, 6, 7, 10	Units 1, 3, 7, 9, 10	All units	All units	All units	All units
recognize some forms and features of texts (L2_com_read.4)	Units 2, 4, 9	Units 2, 4, 7, 9	Units 2, 4, 6, 8, 9	Units 2, 4, 6	Units 2, 4, 5, 8	Units 1, 3, 5, 7, 10
ask questions to seek clarification that develops understanding (L2_com_read.5i)	All units	All units	All units	All units	All units	All units
express opinions and make predictions (L2_com_read.5ii)	Units 1, 3, 6, 8	Units 1, 3	Units 1, 5, 7, 10	Units 1, 8, 9, 10	Units 1, 7, 9, 10	Units 2, 6
YEAR 2						
Level 2						
understand, recount and sequence events and information (L2_com_read.1)	Units 1, 4, 7, 9	Unit 2				Units 1, 5
use a range of reading strategies (L2_com_read.2)	All units	All units	All units	All units	All units	All units
follow discussions, make contributions and observe conventions of conversation (L2_com_talk.2i)	All units	All units	All units	All units	All units	All units
select information for a purpose (L2_com_read.3i)	Units 2, 4, 9	Units 2, 4, 7, 9	Units 2, 4, 6, 8, 9	Units 2, 4, 6	Units 2, 4, 5, 8	Units 1, 3, 5, 7, 10
use basic alphabetical knowledge and visual clues to locate information (L2_com.read.3ii)	Units 1, 2, 3, 4, 5, 6, 7, 10	Units 1, 3, 7, 9, 10	All units	All units	All units	All units
recognise some forms and features of texts (L2_com_read.4)	Units 2, 3, 4, 5, 9, 10	Units 2, 4, 5, 7, 9, 10	Units 2, 4, 6, 8, 9	Units 2, 4, 6	Units 2, 4, 5, 8	Units 1, 3, 5, 7, 10
ask questions to seek clarification that develops understanding (L2_com_read.5i)	All units	All units	All units	All units	All units	All units
express opinions and make predictions (L2_com_read.5ii)	Units 1, 3, 6, 8	Units 1, 3	Units 1, 5, 7, 10	Units 1, 8, 9, 10	Units 1, 7, 9, 10	Units 2, 6

The Cambridge International Primary Curriculum

	Book 1	Book 2	Book 3	Book 4	Book 5	Book 6
STAGE 1						
Demonstrate understanding of explicit meaning in texts						
1Rx1 Read labels, lists and captions to find information.	Units 2, 4, 9	Units 2, 4, 7, 9	Units 2, 4, 6, 8, 9	Units 2, 4, 6	Units 2, 4, 5, 8	Units 1, 3, 5, 7, 10
Demonstrate understanding of implicit meaning in texts						
1Ri1 Anticipate what happens next in a story.	Units 1, 3, 6, 8	Units 1, 3	Units 1, 5, 7, 10	Units 1, 8, 9, 10	Units 1, 7, 9, 10	Units 2, 6
1Ri2 Talk about events in a story and make simple inferences about characters and events to show understanding.	Units 1, 2, 3, 4, 5, 6, 7, 10	Units 1, 3, 7, 9, 10	Units 1, 3, 5, 7, 8, 10	Units 1, 2, 3, 5, 7, 8, 9, 10	Units 1, 2, 3, 6, 7, 8, 9, 10	Units 1, 2, 4, 5, 6, 7, 8, 9
Explain, comment on and analyse the way writers use stylistic and other features of language and structure in texts						
1Rw1 Talk about significant aspects of a story's language, e.g. repetitive refrain, rhyme, patterned language.	Units 3, 5, 10	Units 5, 10				
1Rw2 Recognise story elements, e.g. beginning, middle and end.	Units 1, 4, 7, 9	Unit 2				Units 1, 5
Recognise conventions and evaluate viewpoint, purpose, themes and ideas in texts						
1Rv1 Show awareness that texts for different purposes look different, e.g. use of photographs, diagrams.	Units 2, 4, 9	Units 2, 4, 7, 9	Units 2, 4, 6, 8, 9	Units 2, 4, 6	Units 2, 4, 5, 8	Units 1, 3, 5, 7, 10
1Rv2 Know the parts of a book, e.g. title page, contents.	Units 1, 5	Unit 2	Units 1, 2, 9	Units 3, 4, 7	Unit 8	
STAGE 2						
Demonstrate understanding of explicit meaning in texts						
2Rx1 Read and respond to question words, e.g. *what, where, when, who, why*.	All units	All units	All units	All units	All units	All units
2Rx2 Read and follow simple instructions, e.g. in a recipe.	Unit 4	Unit 2	Unit 6		Unit 4	
2Rx3 Find answers to questions by reading a section of text.	All units	All units	All units	All units	All units	All units
2Rx4 Find factual information from different formats, e.g. charts, labelled diagrams.	Units 2, 4, 9	Units 2, 4, 7, 9	Units 2, 4, 6, 8, 9	Units 2, 4, 6	Units 2, 4, 5, 8	Units 1, 3, 5, 7, 10
Demonstrate understanding of implicit meaning in texts						
2Ri1 Predict story endings.	Units 1, 3, 6, 8	Units 1, 3	Units 1, 5, 7, 10	Units 1, 8, 9, 10	Units 1, 7, 9, 10	Units 2, 6
2Ri2 Identify and describe story settings and characters, recognising that they may be from different times and places.	Units 3, 6, 8	Units 1, 3, 6	Units 1, 5, 7, 10	Units 1, 5, 8, 10	Units 1, 3, 7, 9, 10	Units 2, 6, 8
2Ri3 Make simple inferences from the words on the page, e.g. about feelings.	Units 1, 2, 3, 4, 5, 6, 7, 10	Units 1, 3, 7, 9, 10	Units 1, 3, 5, 7, 8, 10	Units 1, 2, 3, 5, 7, 8, 9, 10	Units 1, 2, 3, 6, 7, 8, 9, 10	Units 1, 2, 4, 5, 6, 7, 8, 9
Explain, comment on and analyse the way writers use stylistic and other features of language and structure in texts						
2Rw1 Comment on some vocabulary choices, e.g. adjectives.	Units 3, 5, 6, 7, 8, 9	Units 1, 3, 4, 6, 7	All units	All units	All units	All units
2Rw2 Talk about what happens at the beginning, in the middle or at the end of a story.	Units 1, 4, 7, 9	Unit 2				Units 1, 5

The Cambridge International Primary Curriculum (cont.)

		Book 1	Book 2	Book 3	Book 4	Book 5	Book 6
2Rw3	Read poems and comment on words and sounds, rhyme and rhythm.	Units 5, 10	Units 5, 10	Unit 3	Unit 3	Unit 6	Units 4, 9
Recognise conventions and evaluate viewpoint, purpose, themes and ideas in texts							
2Rv1	Show some awareness that texts have different purposes.	All units	All units	All units	All units	All units	All units
2Rv2	Identify general features of known text types.	All units	All units	All units	All units	All units	All units

BOOK 1

Book 1 Scope and Sequence

Unit	Pupil Book Focus	Pupil Book texts	Oxford Level	Oxford Reading Criterion Scale link	Genre / text type
1	Events and Characters	*Sophie's Snail*, Dick King-Smith	N/A	standard 2, criteria 2, 3, 9, 10, 12, 14, 21	visual fiction
		Tim's Bedtime	5		
2	Labels and Captions	Farm Fun	6	standard 2, criteria 3, 12, 14, 21, 24	visual non-fiction
		Adam's Visit	5		
3	Patterns in Language	*Henny-Penny*	6	standard 2, criteria 2, 3, 9, 10, 11, 12, 14, 21	fiction using patterned and predictable language
		It Sounds Like an Owl, Hilary Frost & John Jackman	6		
4	Instructions	Banana Split	6	standard 2, criteria 2, 3, 9, 10, 12, 14, 21	visual and written instructions
		Time for a Drink	N/A		
5	Using the Senses	'Cookie Sensations', Tony Mitton	6	standard 2, criteria 2, 3, 9, 10, 11, 12, 14, 21	poetry
		'Five Senses', Moira Andrew	6		
6	Traditional Stories	*Prince Cinders*, Babette Cole	5/6	standard 2, criteria 3, 8, 10, 11, 14, 21, 29	modern and traditional fairy tales
		Cinderella	6		
7	Retelling Events	Our Visit to the Dinosaurs	5/6	standard 2, criteria 3, 14, 21	recounts
		My Naughty Dog!	6		
8	Fantasy Worlds	*The Sandcastle*, M P Robertson	6	standard 2, criteria 3, 14, 21	fantasy fiction
		The Tiger Who Came to Tea, Judith Kerr	6		
9	Information Texts	Being a Friend	6	standard 2, criteria 3, 10, 14, 21	non-fiction
		Sorting Out an Argument	6		
10	Pattern and Rhyme	'Birds in the Garden', Anne English	5	standard 2, criteria 3, 10, 11, 14, 21	poetry
		'The Cow in the Storm', Richard Edwards	5/6		

BOOK 1

Resources & Assessment Book Support	Resources & Assessment Book Extension
word and image matching	drawing and writing about what happens next
cloze activity	describing and drawing
looking at a map and answering questions	describing and drawing
circling the correct answer	providing captions for images
recognising true or false statements	writing about what happens next
recognising the number of times words are used	continuing the story using pattern language
underlining the correct answers	putting items into correct sequence
labelling the picture	writing instructions for a picture
underlining the correct answers	drawing actions for the poem
writing about favourite things to sense	writing a poem
cloze activity	drawing and writing about what happens next
drawing a picture for each sentence	writing about characters' feelings
word and image matching	drawing and writing own recount
putting pictures into correct sequence	drawing and writing about an event
copying the correct answers	identifying fantasy and reality
labelling the picture	drawing and writing fantasy
word and definition matching	writing about what makes a good friend
putting sentences into correct sequence	using personal experience to complete sentences
circling rhyming words, filling the gaps	using personal experience to answer questions
putting pictures into correct sequence	writing about preferred poem

17

BOOK 1 — UNIT 1

UNIT FOCUS: Events and Characters

Investigating ...
- recalling events
- prediction
- visualisation
- drawing on their own experience

TEACH/TALK

- Ask the children to look carefully at the pictures in the Pupil Book and discuss what happened.
- Talk about the terms **setting**, **character** and **event** in relation to the story.
- Read and answer the questions as a class or in groups.

RESOURCES & ASSESSMENT BOOK

- **Support:** (comprehension support) linking lines to match pictures to text.
- **Extension:** predicting what happens next; draw a picture and describe. Linked to Pupil Book Q8: *What do you think happens next?* Children are required to draw a picture of what they think happens next and write a sentence about it. Remind the children to start their sentence with a capital letter and end with a full stop.

PUPIL BOOK ANSWERS

1. Sophie.
2. In the evening.
3. In the bathroom of Sophie's house.
4. The snail was put on the side of the sink, but Sophie accidentally knocked it into the water where it was sucked down the plug hole.
5. Three words that rhyme with snail: e.g. hail, pail, tail, tale, sale, pale, male.
6. Answer that suggests that Sophie is unhappy/upset.
7. Answer that suggests that Sophie has befriended the snail.
8. Child's own response detailing what may happen next.

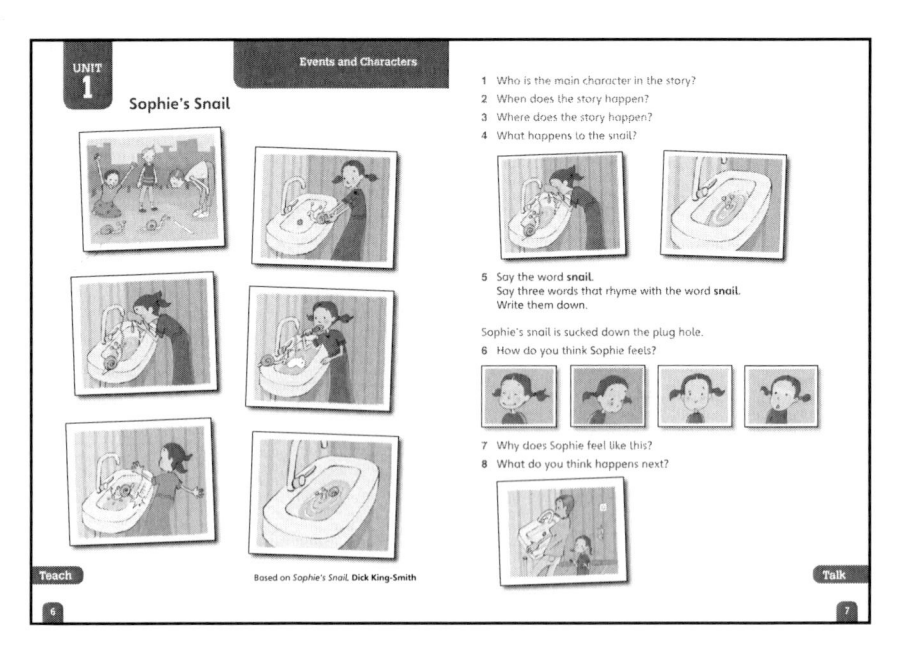

RESOURCE SHEET ANSWERS

Support

Picture 1: Sophie puts the snail on the sink.
Picture 2: Sophie washes her face.
Picture 3: Sophie brushes her teeth.
Picture 4: The snail falls into the water.

Extension
Individual answers.

GOING DEEPER

- Review the children's answers to the questions. If they struggle to identify the main character and setting they can be encouraged to find evidence by looking carefully at the pictures.
- Discuss how they used their own experiences to answer the questions and to understand Sophie's feelings.

BOOK 1

UNIT 1

WRITE

- Children look at the short passage that shows in words and pictures what Tim does at bedtime. This extract should be used for small group or individual work.
- The questions in this section establish whether children can identify the main elements in this extract. Ask the children to answer the questions individually, then review their answers.

RESOURCES & ASSESSMENT BOOK

- **Support:** (comprehension support) fill the gaps.
- **Extension:** children describe and draw what they do at bedtime. Linked to Pupil Book Q6: *Write three things you do before you get into bed.* Discuss with the children things they do before they go to bed each night. Encourage them to write simple sentences. Introduce the words *first*, *then* and *finally*, explaining how they help to show the order in which things are done.

PUPIL BOOK ANSWERS

1. Tim fills the sink.
2. Yes.
3. He pulls out the plug.
4. Three naming words in *Tim's Bedtime*: e.g. water, face, teeth, plug, bed.
5. The title 'Tim's Bedtime' and the fact Tim is in his pyjamas tell us that Tim is not getting ready in the morning but in the evening. After Tim pulls out the plug he goes to bed.
6. Child's own answer detailing three things they do before getting into bed each night. Encourage the child to write simple sentences. Introduce the words *first*, *then* and *finally*, explaining how they help to show the order in which things are done.

RESOURCE SHEET ANSWERS

Support

1. I fill the sink with *water*.
2. I wash my *face*.
3. I brush my *teeth*.
4. I pull out the *plug* and then go to *bed*.

Extension
Individual answers.

GOING DEEPER

- Review children's answers to the questions. They can then recount the events based on their own experience, reading aloud their three simple sentences or showing their pictures.
- Children can compare their experiences by standing in groups to show how many children brush their teeth first, how many children read a book and so on.

BOOK 1 — UNIT 2

UNIT FOCUS: Labels and Captions

Investigating ...
- using labels, captions and lists
- consolidating children's understanding that writing carries meaning
- helping children develop the concept of a sentence

TEACH/TALK

- Look at labels around the classroom and ask children to explain why something may have been given a label, e.g. scissors.
- Look at the Farm Fun map. Ask the children to highlight things they notice.
- Ask the children to read the labels on the map. Discuss the items with captions, highlighting the extra information these provide for the reader and the fact that they are written in sentences.
- Read and answer the questions as a class or in groups.

RESOURCES & ASSESSMENT BOOK

- **Support:** (comprehension support) look at the map and answer questions.
- **Extension:** draw pictures and write sentences to show what you would like to do at the farm. Linked to Pupil Book Q8: *What would you like to do at the farm?*

  Children draw three pictures and write a sentence for each one. Encourage them to add detail to their sentences, e.g. expanding 'I am feeding the sheep.' to 'I enjoy feeding the hungry sheep.'

PUPIL BOOK ANSWERS

1. Toys and small gifts.
2. From the café.
3. Rabbits, goats and sheep.
4. There are five types of animals on the Farm Walk: hens, cows, ponies, sheep and goats.
5. boats: goats, sleep: sheep, pens: hens
6. A caption tells us that the Farm Walk takes an hour.
7. Answer that suggests which areas children may enjoy the most.
8. Child's own answer suggesting what they would enjoy doing at the farm, should they want to go.

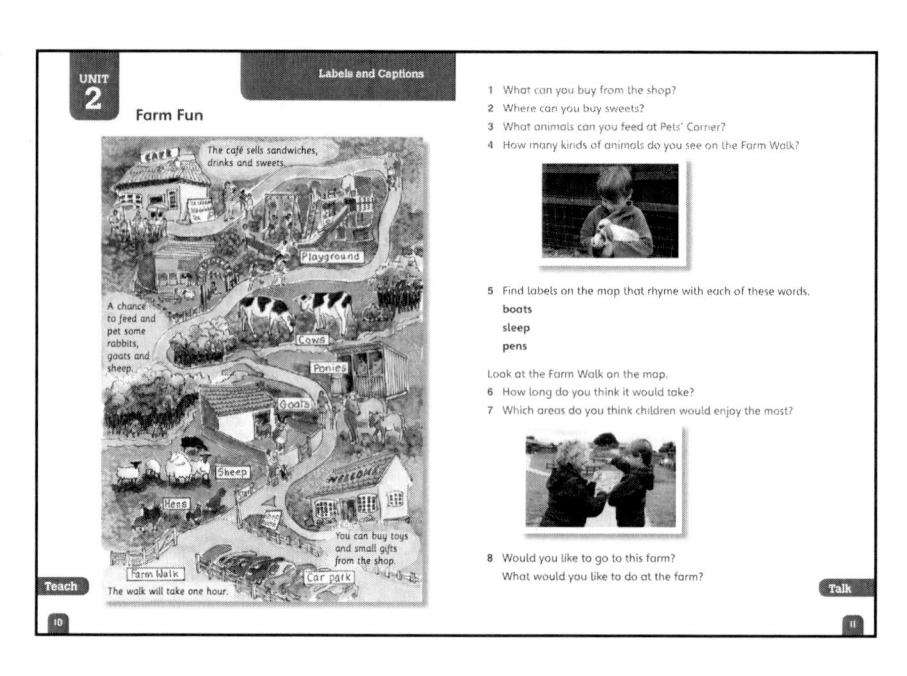

RESOURCE SHEET ANSWERS

Support

1. two
2. five
3. eight
4. four
5. one
6. one
7. four
8. one

Extension
Individual answers.

GOING DEEPER

- Review the children's answers to the questions. Ensure they can identify the different ways that information can be transformed from the map into knowledge, e.g. labels and captions. Encourage those who struggle with words to find evidence by looking carefully at the pictures.

BOOK 1   UNIT 2

WRITE

- Ask the children to work in small groups or on their own and look at the photographs with captions.
- Ask them to answer the questions. Remind them that for the red questions they need to copy the whole sentence in answer to the question.
- Ask the children to answer the questions individually, then review their answers.

RESOURCES & ASSESSMENT BOOK

- **Support:** (comprehension support) circle the correct answer.
- **Extension:** look at the pictures and write what Adam is doing. Linked to Pupil Book Q6: *Two pictures need a sentence each.* Children should think about a caption for the two pictures. Words are provided to help. Encourage them to write simple sentences, reminding them to use a capital letter and a full stop.

PUPIL BOOK ANSWERS

1. Adam sits outside the café.
2. Adam feeds the goats.
3. Adam plays on the swings.
4. Adam, cows, lunch
5. Individual answers that suggest they have looked at the evidence in the photos, e.g. Adam is seen smiling in the photos; Adam looks like he is having lots of fun, to decide if Adam enjoyed his day out.
6. Two pictures need a sentence. Children should think about a caption for the two pictures. Encourage them to write simple sentences, reminding them to use a capital letter and a full stop.

RESOURCE SHEET ANSWERS

Support
1. cows
2. sandwich
3. boots
4. milk
5. yes

Extension
Individual answers.

GOING DEEPER

- Ask the children to write a list of what Adam and his family should take to the farm. The pictures in the Pupil Book will help children who need more support. How do their lists vary?
- Children then recount what they would like to do at the farm.
- Conclude by summarising the use of labels, lists and captions. Brainstorm other times when they may be used.

BOOK 1 UNIT 3

UNIT FOCUS: Patterns in Language

Investigating ...
- patterned language in stories
- how patterned language: makes writing more memorable
  gives characters catchphrases
  gives the story pace

TEACH/TALK

- Read the extract to or with the children, either in groups or as a class.
- Discuss the following terms in the context of the extract: **setting**, **character** and **event**.
- Highlight the characters' names and how they give the reader a clue as to which animal they may be.
- Answer the questions with the children.
- Encourage the children to feel empathy with Henny-Penny. Would they feel the same in the same situation? If not, why not?
- Discuss the pattern of the story so far. What happens each time another animal is met?

RESOURCES & ASSESSMENT BOOK

- **Support:** (comprehension support) recognising true or false statements.
- **Extension:** predicting what will happen next. Linked to Pupil Book Q8: *What do you think will happen next?* Children are required to draw two pictures and write about each one. Brainstorm different scenarios or encourage children to think of unexpected outcomes on their own.

PUPIL BOOK ANSWERS

1. An acorn.
2. That the sky was falling.
3. To see the King.
4. Goosey-Poosey.
5. 'Goodness gracious.'
6. Answer that suggests that Goosey-Poosey may have asked 'Where are you going?' to Henny-Penny and the others.
7. Answer that suggests that Goosey-Poosey also wanted to go to tell the King.
8. Child's own suggestion about what may have happened when the animals met a fox.

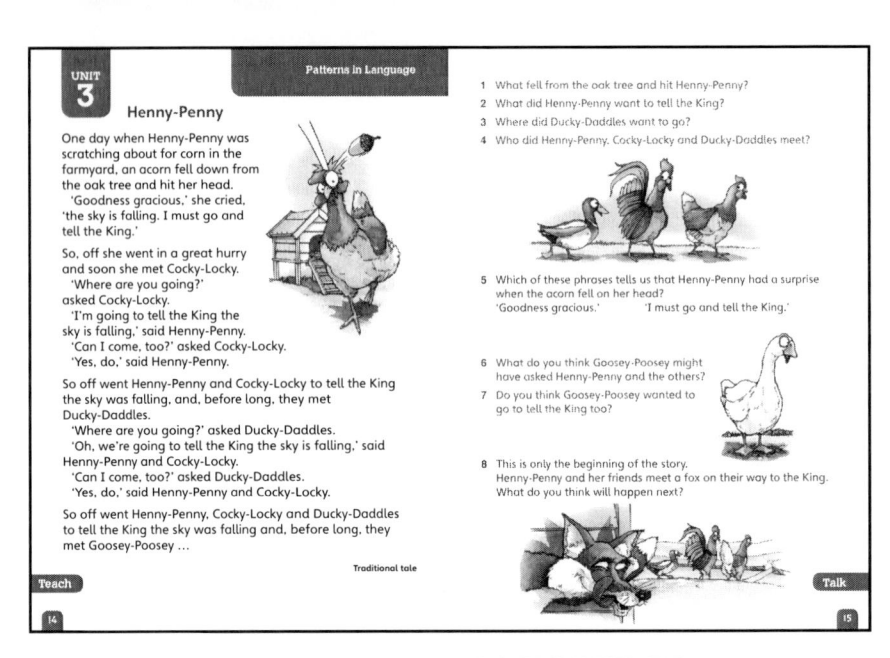

RESOURCE SHEET ANSWERS

Support
1. false
2. true
3. true
4. false
5. true
6. true

Extension
Individual answers.

GOING DEEPER

- Discuss the pattern used in this story and what predictably happens each time another animal is met.
- Ask the children to make up a character of their own and then use the pattern of the story to write/say what happens when their character is met by Henny-Penny. This can either be done individually or in groups. Share the results with the rest of the class.

BOOK 1 — UNIT 3

WRITE

- Ask the children to read the extract on their own or in small groups.
- Ask the children to answer the questions, then review their answers.
- Remind them that for the red questions they need to copy the whole sentence in answer to the question.

RESOURCES & ASSESSMENT BOOK

- **Support:** (comprehension support) recognising the number of times words are used.
- **Extension:** continuing the story using the same pattern. Linked to Pupil Book Q8: *Choose your own animals and names to continue the story*. The patterned structure of the story can be highlighted using this resource sheet. It is easy for the child to see the few words that vary. Animal prompts are given but children may like to choose any animal.

PUPIL BOOK ANSWERS

1. Ben is worried by the howl.
2. Pen thinks the howl is an owl.
3. Sue tells Ben to go to sleep.
4. It is Spot howling.
5. E.g. *Howl ... Howl ...*
   'What's that sound? What's that loud sound?'
   'Go to sleep, Ben!'
6. Answer that gives how many times the line the child chose for Q5 is repeated in the poem.
7. Answer that suggests how the child may feel if they heard the howling while camping.
8. Children are required to use the patterned language from the extract while introducing animals of their own choice into the story

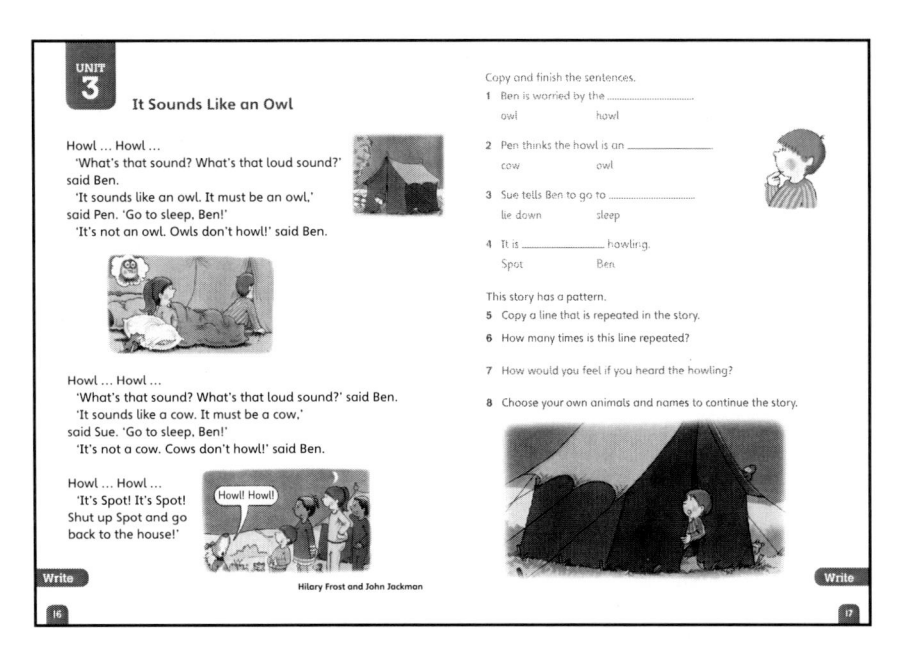

RESOURCE SHEET ANSWERS

Support

1. Howl is used three times.
2. Owl is used three times (four if 'owls' included).
3. Sound is used two times (three if 'sounds' included).
4. Ben is used three times.
5. Said is used three times.

Extension

Individual answers.

GOING DEEPER

- Encourage children to read aloud their own versions of patterned language from their answers to question 8 in the Pupil Book.
- Children can work in small groups to role-play the story, repeating the key elements of the patterns used.

BOOK 1

UNIT 4

UNIT FOCUS: Instructions

Investigating ...
- the role of instructions
- how instructions differ from descriptive sentences

TEACH/TALK

- Give the children a set of simple instructions to follow, such as moving from the carpet to their desks, picking up a pencil on the way.
  - Call out the instructions in stages rather than as a general request, so the children can understand what a series of instructions is like.
  - Ask the children to repeat the instructions you have just given them. Highlight the fact that instructions are given or written in an impersonal way.
- Look at the *Banana Split* pictures in the Pupil Book, either as a class or in groups. Discuss and answer the questions with the children.

RESOURCES & ASSESSMENT BOOK

- **Support:** (comprehension support) underline the correct answers.
- **Extension:** put the items into the correct order. Linked to Pupil Book Q4: *Write the food in the order you will need it*. Challenge children to complete this exercise from memory.

PUPIL BOOK ANSWERS

1. Peel the banana and cut it down the middle, from the top to the bottom.
   Put the banana on a plate and put the ice cream on top of it.
   Pour the chocolate sauce over the banana and ice cream.
   Put the strawberries and chocolate chips on the top.

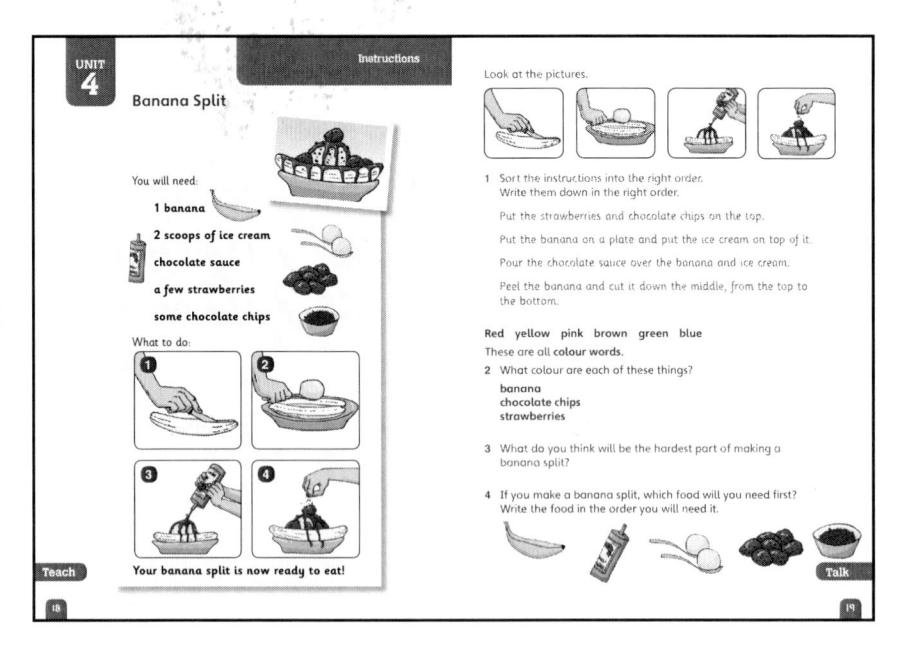

2. banana = yellow, chocolate chips = brown, strawberries = red

3. Answer that suggests what the child will find the hardest part of making the banana split, e.g. cutting the banana.

4. Order of the items that are used in the recipe: banana, ice cream, chocolate sauce, strawberries and chocolate chips

RESOURCE SHEET ANSWERS

Support

1. Cut the banana.
2. In a bowl.
3. Chocolate sauce
4. At the end.

Extension

banana, ice cream, chocolate sauce, strawberries and chocolate chips

GOING DEEPER

- Work through the children's answers and recap to ensure they can identify the way instructions are written differently from descriptive sentences.
- Discuss with the children how the Banana Split recipe might be changed, e.g. remove chocolate chips and add marshmallows. Illustrate how the instructions would change. Ask the children to invent and write simple instructions for their own Banana Split recipe, adding things they would love to eat with the banana.

BOOK 1

UNIT 4

WRITE

- Ask the children to work as individuals or in small groups and look at the illustrations in *Time for a Drink*. Encourage them to look carefully in order to extract the relevant information.
- Ask the children to answer all the questions individually. Remind them that for red questions they need to copy out the whole sentence, filling in the missing word.

RESOURCES & ASSESSMENT BOOK

- **Support:** (comprehension support) label the picture.
- **Extension:** write instructions for each picture. Linked to Pupil Book Q7: *Write instructions for each picture.* Remind the children of the different writing style needed for instructions. Some words have been provided to give support in the spelling of words, as well as helping support the children's ideas. This exercise brings together all the elements of information needed in order to provide appropriate instructions for making a glass of squash.

PUPIL BOOK ANSWERS

1. The boy is making a *drink*.
2. He pours juice into a *glass*.
3. The boy adds water from the *jug*.
4. He *drinks* the glass of squash.
5. glass, water, squash, jug. Children who struggle with this task could draw the items instead of listing them.
6. Answer that suggests the pictures show the boy is making the drink carefully by the expression on his face and the fact he hasn't spilt anything.
7. The child's own instructions detailing how to make the drink, including the words provided to help.

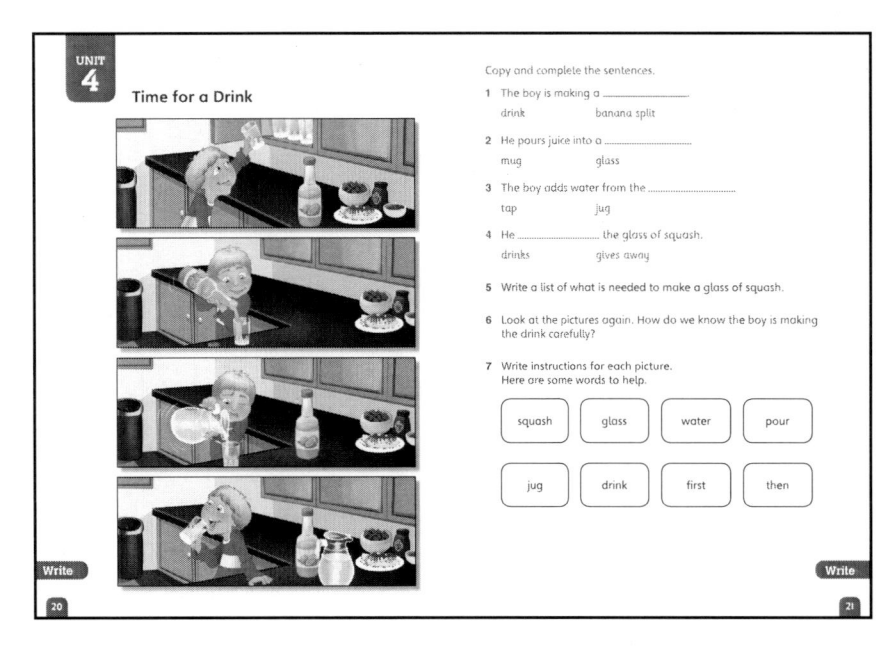

RESOURCE SHEET ANSWERS

Support

jug, water, juice, glass, drink

Extension

Individual instructions.

GOING DEEPER

- As a class or in groups review the children's answers. Compare the different ways the instructions to the drink activity have been written.
- Divide the children into pairs and ask them to write short instructions for other activities of their choice, e.g. brushing their teeth. Ask them to try out the instructions to see if they work well.
- Summarise the use of instructions. Brainstorm other times when instructions may be used.

BOOK 1 UNIT 5

UNIT FOCUS: Using the Senses

Investigating ...
- reading and responding to poems that capture sensory experiences
- exploring children's own senses and finding words that describe their experiences

TEACH/TALK

- Read the poem 'Cookie Sensations' to the class.
- Revise the five senses and discuss the senses in this poem. You may like to give children a cookie to eat whilst discussing the words used to describe the cookie in the poem. What words would children use to describe the cookie they are eating?
- Encourage children to read the poem aloud together, following the rhythm and keeping time.
- Discuss the poem and answer the questions together.

RESOURCES & ASSESSMENT BOOK

- **Support:** (comprehension support) underline the correct answers.
- **Extension:** draw actions to accompany the poem. Linked to Pupil Book Q8: *Think of actions for the poem.* Ask the children to split the verses into separate actions. They will need to try out various actions before deciding on the best one for each verse.

PUPIL BOOK ANSWERS

1. The poem is about a cookie that is seen in a shop window.
2. Because the girl says that her mouth starts to water when she sees the cookie.
3. Yes, the cookie smells so nice the girl says it drives her mad wanting to eat it.
4. The cookie tastes sweet.
5. pop
6. sweet
7. Answer that suggests the girl feels happy after eating the cookie.
8. The children are asked to devise actions they could do while reciting the poem.

RESOURCE SHEET ANSWERS

Support

1. In the baker's shop.
2. A paper bag.
3. crunchy
4. Child's own response to whether they would like to eat the cookie.
5. Words that describe the cookie: crunchy, tasty, sweet, crumbly.

Extension

Individual responses.

GOING DEEPER

- As a class or in groups, review children's answers to the questions.
- Encourage groups or pairs to perform the poem using the actions they have chosen, reciting the poem clearly.

BOOK 1   UNIT 5

WRITE

- Ask the children to read the poem in small groups or as individuals.
- Ask them to answer the questions individually, then review their answers. Encourage them to write in whole sentences.

RESOURCES & ASSESSMENT BOOK

- **Support:** (comprehension support) write down things they like to taste, smell, feel, hear or see.
- **Extension:** write a poem about things they don't like. Linked to Pupil Book Q6: *Write a poem about things you don't like.*

PUPIL BOOK ANSWERS

1. The taste of toothpaste.
2. The sound of bells.
3. The fairground lights flashing.
4. Pictures drawn by the child representing each of the five senses.
5. The children are asked to list five things they like that relate to the five senses.
6. The children are asked to write a poem about things they don't like that relate to the five senses. Introduce and discuss similes for 'like' and 'don't like', the latter often evoking more powerful feelings.

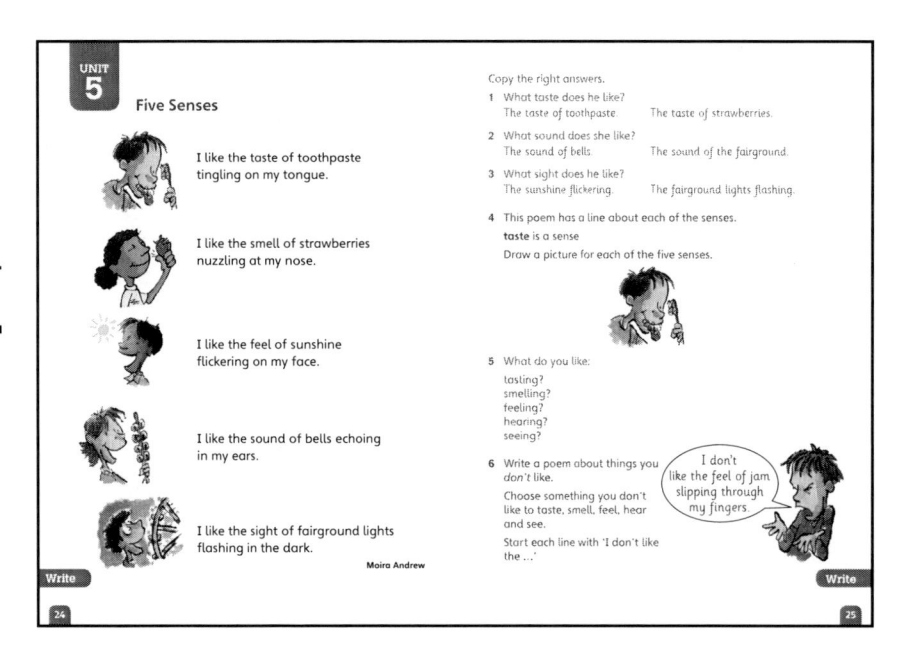

RESOURCE SHEET ANSWERS

Support
This resource sheet can be used to organise the children's ideas into the different sense categories describing things they like.

Extension
Individual poems.

GOING DEEPER

- As a class or group, review the children's answers, encouraging the children to discuss their own experiences and notice how these differ from other people's.
- Ask the children to read their poems aloud.

BOOK 1   UNIT 6

UNIT FOCUS: Traditional Stories
Investigating ...
- traditional stories
- characters, plot and events

TEACH/TALK

- Ask the children to look carefully at the picture story in the Pupil Book.
- Discuss the following terms in the context of the extract: **setting**, **character** and **event**.
- Introduce the voice of the story as the 'narrator'. Then discuss the setting, characters and events in relation to the extract.
- Answer the questions as a class or in groups.

RESOURCES & ASSESSMENT BOOK

- **Support:** (comprehension support) complete the sentences.
- **Extension:** draw pictures and predict what happens next. Links to Pupil Book Q8: *What happens next to Prince Cinders?* It is important that the children make the link between this story and the more traditional story of *Cinderella*.

PUPIL BOOK ANSWERS

1. No
2. Three
3. Answers that suggest the brothers went out to the ball.
4. A soot-covered fairy.
5. E.g. scruffy, dirty, small, thin, hard-working, sad
6. Cinderella
7. Answer to suggest the child is able to make links between this story and the fairy-tale version of *Cinderella*, e.g. brothers go off to ball leaving Prince Cinders working/sisters go off to ball leaving Cinderella working, etc.
8. Child's own interpretation of what happens next but recognising the link with the fairy tale *Cinderella* and mimicking what happens in that fairy tale.

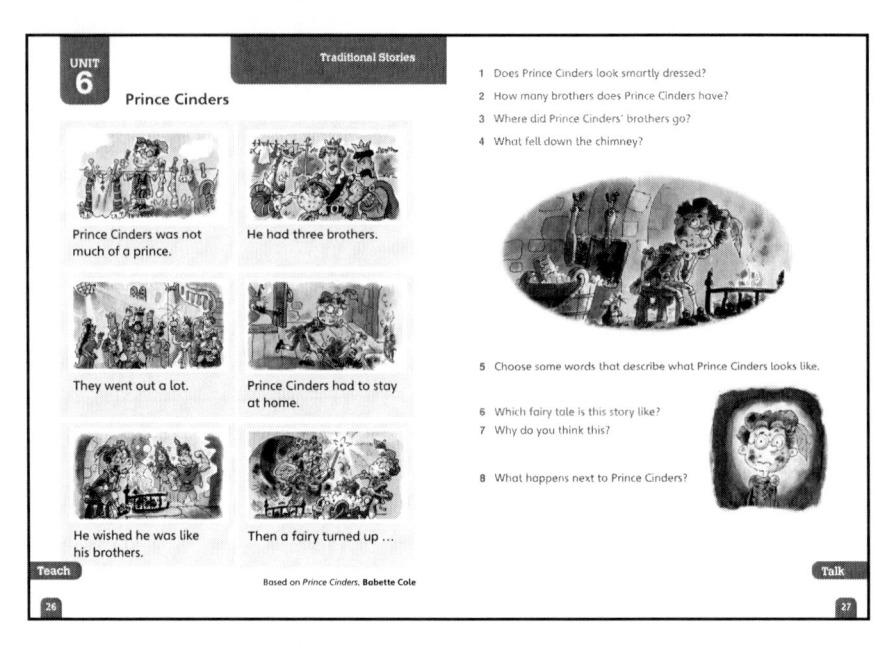

RESOURCE SHEET ANSWERS

Support
Child to choose appropriate words from those given to complete each sentence.

Extension
Individual answers.

GOING DEEPER

- Recap the different descriptive words the children have found to describe Prince Cinders.
- Did the children enjoy this new version of *Cinderella*? Why or why not? Obtain a copy of the book *Prince Cinders* and read the actual end of the story.

BOOK 1
UNIT 6

WRITE

- Ask the children to read the *Cinderella* playscript extract as individuals or in small groups.
- Ask them to answer the questions individually. Remind them that for the red questions they need to copy out the complete sentence.
- Review their answers.
- Highlight the difference between a playscript and a normal story. Discuss the importance of the narrator's role.

RESOURCES & ASSESSMENT BOOK

- **Support:** (comprehension support) draw a picture for each sentence.
- **Extension:** complete the table to show how Cinderella and her sisters feel. Linked to Pupil Book Q6: *How do you think Cinderella and the ugly sisters feel at different times in the story?* This requires the children to be aware of the traditional *Cinderella* story. It asks the children to look at the main characters (Cinderella and her sisters) in more detail and follow how they may be feeling at different stages in the story.

PUPIL BOOK ANSWERS

1. She wanted to go to the ball.
2. Her godmother helped.
3. She danced with the prince.
4. No, she didn't leave on time.
5. Answer that suggests a 'ball' can be a round object that is fun to play with, or a game ('playing ball').
6. Answers that suggest that the main characters, Cinderella and the ugly sisters, have opposing feelings at different times, e.g. Cinderella is delighted when the shoe fits but the ugly sisters are not!
7. Children's opinions on which of the two stories they liked the best, in the form of a sentence.

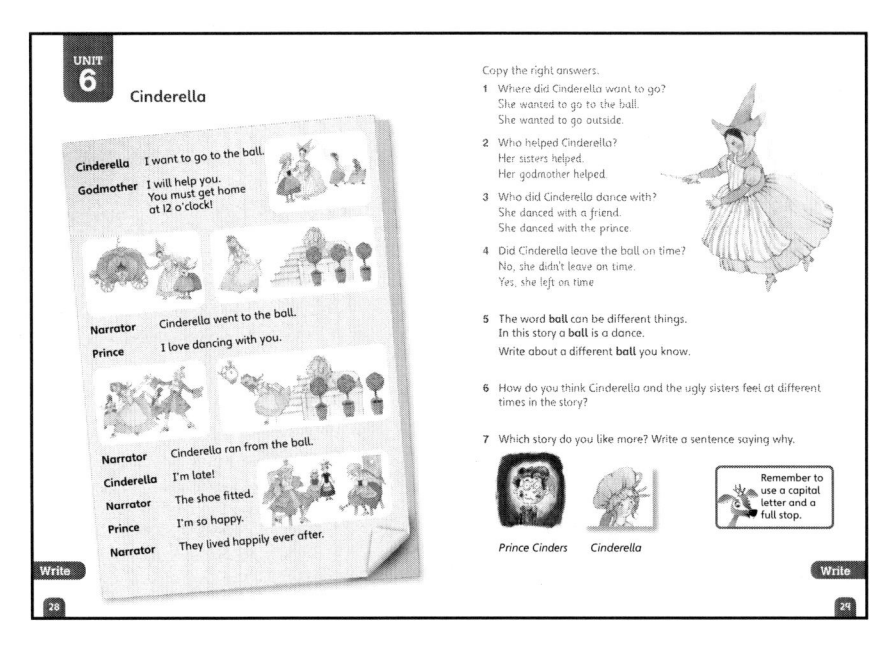

RESOURCE SHEET ANSWERS

Support
Pictures drawn by the child representing each stage of the *Cinderella* story.

Extension
Individual answers.

GOING DEEPER

- Discuss as a larger group which story was preferred. Ask children to arrange themselves into two groups to show which story was more popular.
- In small groups children can re-enact the *Cinderella* play, or a new, completed version of *Prince Cinders*.

BOOK 1

UNIT 7

UNIT FOCUS: Retelling Events

Investigating ...
- recalling something that has happened and ordering events
- writing in the past tense and using time connectives

TEACH/TALK

- Give the children a recount of something that happened recently in class. Ask them, if they were to write it up, whether it would be a piece of fiction or non-fiction.
- Ask children to recount something orally. Act as scribe. Discuss the importance of ordering events and using time connectives, e.g. *First, Next, After,* etc.
- Discuss with children the fact that recounts are written in the past tense.
- Look at the comic strip in the Pupil Book with the children. Ask them to answer the questions to help reinforce their understanding of how a recount may be written.

RESOURCES & ASSESSMENT BOOK

- **Support:** (comprehension support) linking lines to match the pictures to the correct text.
- **Extension:** illustrate their own visit and write a recount. Linked to Pupil Book Q7: *Where have you been on a visit?* Children are asked to draw a picture and then write a recount about the visit. Remind the children to use connectives, encouraging them to think of the order things happened in.

PUPIL BOOK ANSWERS

1. At the museum.
2. He felt sick/unwell.
3. The moving dinosaurs.
4. Three horns.
5. E.g. frightening, big, huge, strong, strange.
6. Answer that suggests the boy in the final picture (Jake) enjoyed the trip and why the children think that is the case.
7. Details of visits the children have made.

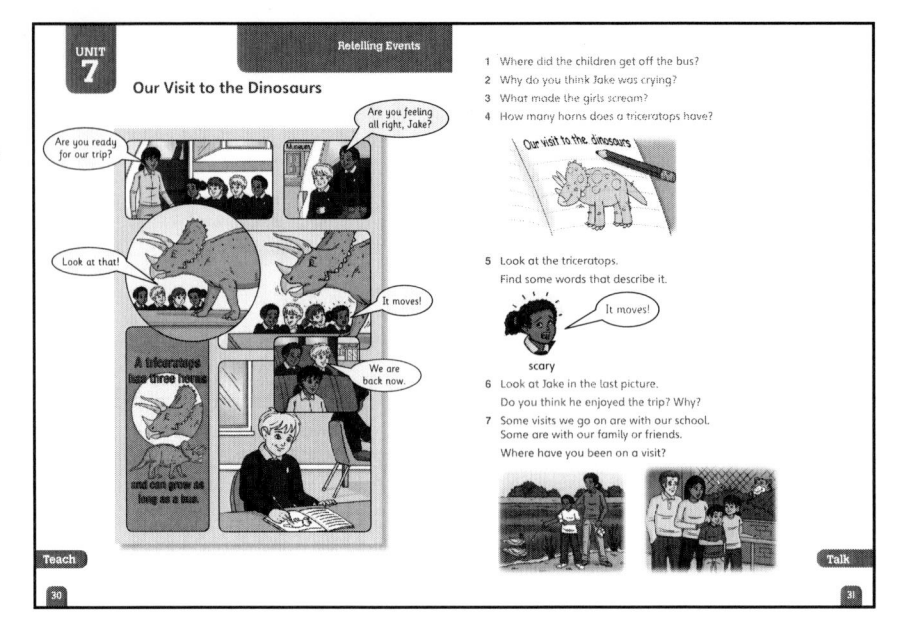

RESOURCE SHEET SUPPORT ANSWERS

Support
Sentences linked to correct pictures with a line.

Extension
Individual answers.

GOING DEEPER

- Ask children to share their recounts of their own visit. If any children have written about the same event or place, compare their recounts to show how different people have different perspectives on the same activities.

BOOK 1

UNIT 7

WRITE

- Ask children to work individually or in small groups to read the extract.
- Ask children to answer the questions individually. Review their answers.

RESOURCES & ASSESSMENT BOOK

- **Support:** number the pictures to show the correct order of events. This resource sheet extends the recount of Barney and the chewed shoes. Children are asked to look at four further pictures that detail what happened next. They are required to number the pictures in the correct order.
- **Extension:** illustrate and write about an event. Linked to Pupil Book Q7: *Think of something that has happened between you and an animal.* This resource sheet helps the child structure their recount. Remind all children to write each sentence correctly, using a capital letter and ending with a full stop.

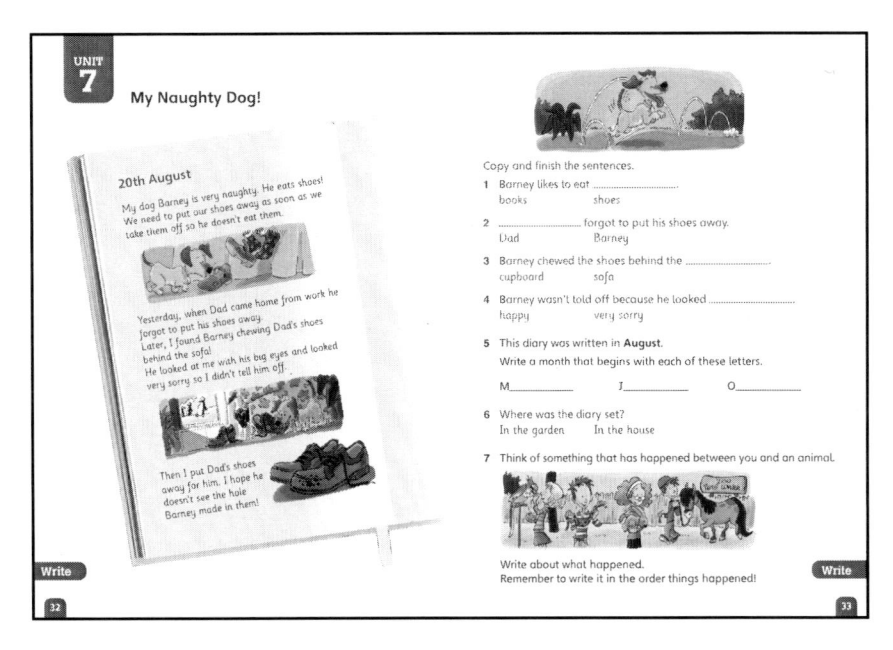

PUPIL BOOK ANSWERS

1. Barney likes to eat *shoes*.
2. *Dad* forgot to put his shoes away.
3. Barney chewed the shoes behind the *sofa*.
4. Barney wasn't told off because he looked *very sorry*.
5. M: March, May;
   J: January, June, July;
   O: October (Only one answer per letter is required.)
6. In the house.
7. Child's own recount of something that happened between them and an animal.

RESOURCE SHEET ANSWERS

Support

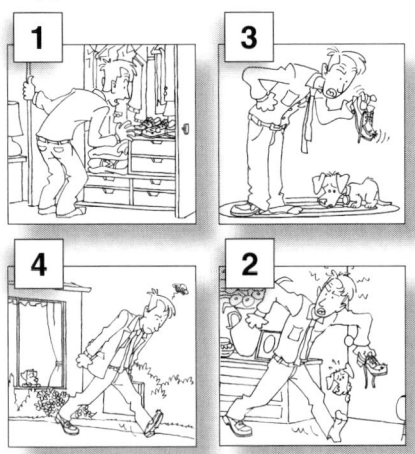

Extension
Individual answers.

GOING DEEPER

- Summarise the purpose of recounts, reminding children that they are written in the past tense and use time connectives.

BOOK 1

UNIT 8

UNIT FOCUS: Fantasy Worlds
Investigating ...
- characters, plot and events
- stories about fantasy worlds compared to reality and personal experience

TEACH/TALK

- Read the extract from *The Sandcastle* as a class.
- Revisit the following terms: **setting**, **character** and **event**.
- Discuss the setting of the story and Jack, the main character.
- Check the children's understanding of the extract by asking further questions. What did Jack put on the castle he built on the beach? Do you think the shell had anything to do with Jack's wishes? What happened to the people when the water came in?
- Answer the questions with the children.

RESOURCES & ASSESSMENT BOOK

- **Support:** (comprehension support) copy the right answers.
- **Extension:** circle the things that would never happen. Linked to Pupil Book Q6: *Which things wouldn't happen to you in real life?*

PUPIL BOOK ANSWERS

1. Sandcastles.
2. King of the castle.
3. A girl.
4. The sea (water).
5. football, bedroom

6. Strange things that happened in the story:
   It is unlikely you would see a castle outside your bedroom window.
   You wouldn't be made king.
   The people wouldn't change when they found themselves in water.

7. Individual answers about what happens next to Jack and how the story finishes.

RESOURCE SHEET SUPPORT ANSWERS

Support

1. Jack likes building sandcastles.
2. Jack wants to be a king.
3. Jack met a girl.
4. Water came in the castle doors.

Extension

The following circled:
Jack goes into the big sandcastle.
Jack was made king.

GOING DEEPER

- Ask children to share their endings to the story. Role-play some of the story endings.
- Obtain a copy of the book *The Sandcastle* to read the actual ending of the story to the children.

BOOK 1 · UNIT 8

WRITE

- Ask children to read the extract individually or in small groups.
- Ask children to answer the questions individually.

RESOURCES & ASSESSMENT BOOK

- **Support:** (comprehension support) label the picture.
- **Extension:** draw pictures and write sentences to explain what the children would do if a tiger came for tea. Linked to Pupil Book Q7: *If a tiger knocked at your door what would you do?* The children are required to write their own story based on a similar situation, but anything can happen!

PUPIL BOOK ANSWERS

1. Sophie was having tea with her mummy.
2. Sophie heard a ring.
3. Sophie opened the door.
4. The tiger wanted to have tea.
5. Sophie: pretty, polite, small
   Tiger: furry, big, stripy, hungry, polite
   This activity requires the children to look more closely at the characters. Discuss the word 'polite' and why that can be linked to both characters.
6. E.g. surprised, terrified, excited.
7. The children are asked to imagine they are the one who opened the door to the tiger. What would happen in the story if they were the main character?

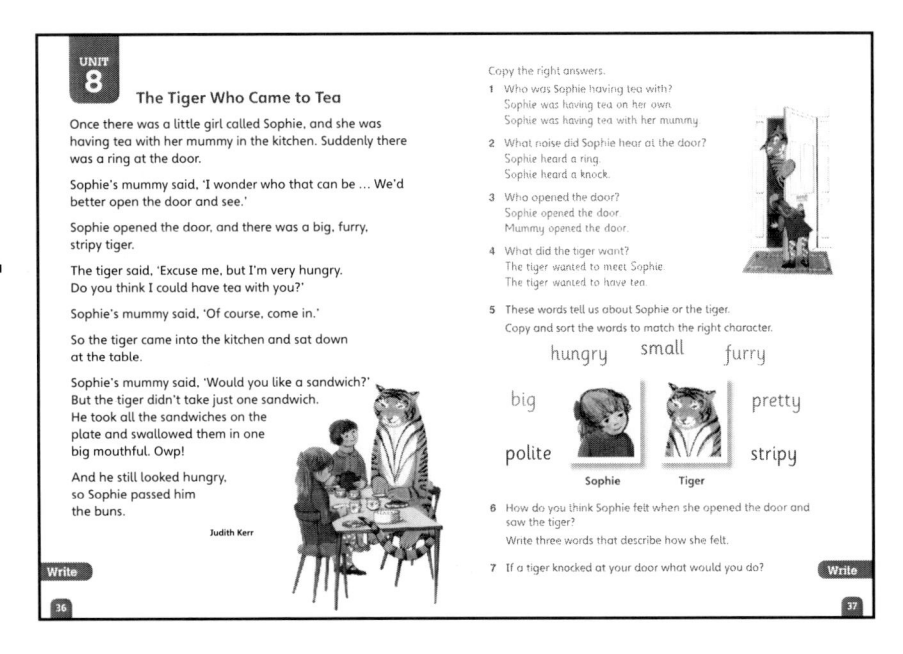

RESOURCE SHEET ANSWERS

Support

Labels: Mummy, Sophie, tiger, jug, table, cup, cake

Extension
Individual answers.

GOING DEEPER

- Review children's answers to the questions. Discuss whether children like fantasy stories and why.
- Share the children's stories of a tiger knocking on their door.
- Create an imaginary setting with the class and, in groups, ask children to explore story ideas, possibly through role-play.

BOOK 1 — UNIT 9

UNIT FOCUS: Information Texts

Investigating ...
- non-fiction texts
- how different texts can provide information

TEACH/TALK

- Discuss how the text is organised: information is given under sub-headings to make reference to the information easier.
- Read through the text with the class or in groups.
- Read, discuss and answer the questions with the children.
- Ask the children to look more closely at the information in each section. Highlight how they need to look for picture or written clues to help guide them to the appropriate sections.

RESOURCES & ASSESSMENT BOOK

- **Support:** (vocabulary support) linking lines to match the words to their meanings. If necessary, read the words and definitions to the children.
- **Extension:** draw and write about friends. Linked to Pupil Book Q6: *Write about two of your friends.* This resource sheet should promote discussion about what makes a good friend. Brainstorm with the children words they may use to describe their friends. Encourage children to put their thoughts into sentences.

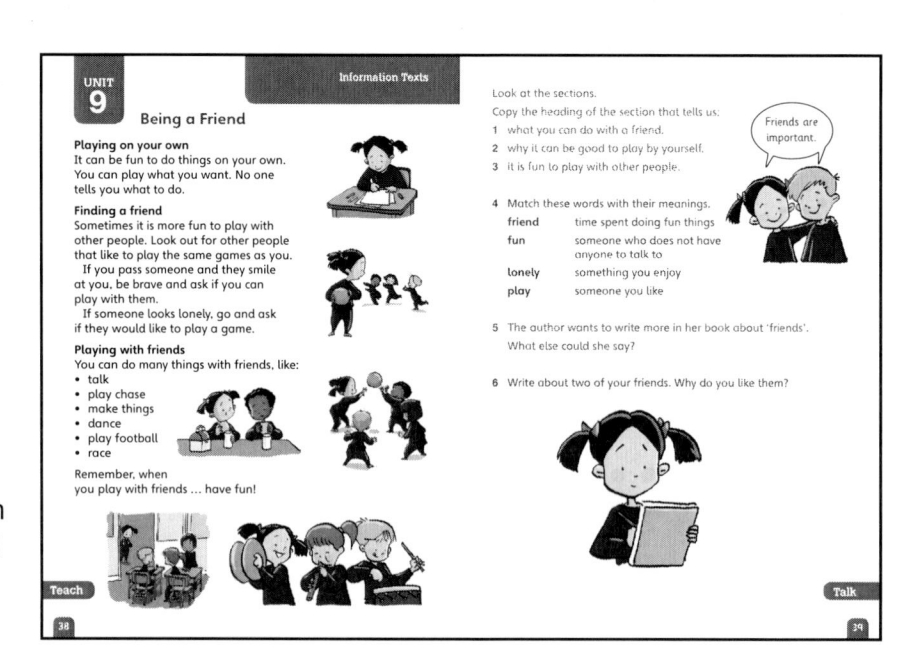

PUPIL BOOK ANSWERS

1. Playing with friends.
2. Playing on your own.
3. Finding a friend.
4. friend – someone you like
   play – time spent doing fun things
   lonely – someone who does not have anyone to talk to
   fun – something you enjoy
5. Answer that suggests what else the author may include in her book, e.g. Playing in groups, Games to play with friends, How to sort out an argument.
6. Individual answers about two friends and why the child likes them.

RESOURCE SHEET ANSWERS

Support

brave: being strong inside
help: doing something to make someone feel better
game: a fun activity
on your own: by yourself
shy: someone who is afraid to meet or speak to anyone

Extension

Individual answers.

GOING DEEPER

- Recap to ensure that the children can identify the different ways information texts are laid out.
- Discuss in more detail how to find a friend. Ask children to order their ideas with the most important points first.
- Share the children's ideas of what else may be added to a class book on friendship. What makes the children good friends?

BOOK 1

UNIT 9

WRITE

- Ask children to work individually or in small groups, and look carefully at the pictures and text in *Sorting Out an Argument* in order to extract the relevant information.
- Ask children to answer the questions individually. Remind them that for the red questions they need to copy out the whole sentence.

RESOURCES & ASSESSMENT BOOK

- **Support:** (comprehension support) order the steps by numbering sentences. Children can refer to the Pupil Book if necessary.
- **Extension:** complete the sentences using personal experience. Linked to Pupil Book Q8: *Have you ever argued with a friend?* This resource sheet gives a structure to answering this question and points from which pairs or groups of children could discuss their answers before writing about them individually.

PUPIL BOOK ANSWERS

1. This *information* tells us what to do if we have an argument.
2. The first thing you should do is *stop* arguing.
3. *Everyone* must have a turn to tell their story.
4. Choose the best *idea* to solve the argument.
5. tell, yell
6. E.g. bell, sell, fell, shell, etc.
7. Answer that suggests the children have thought about the information and whether it may work in their own situation.
8. The children are asked to write about an argument they have had. Encourage the children to think about an argument they have had with a friend and ask them to write a few sentences explaining how the argument was sorted out. Some children may be able to provide detail, possibly ordering and numbering what happened.

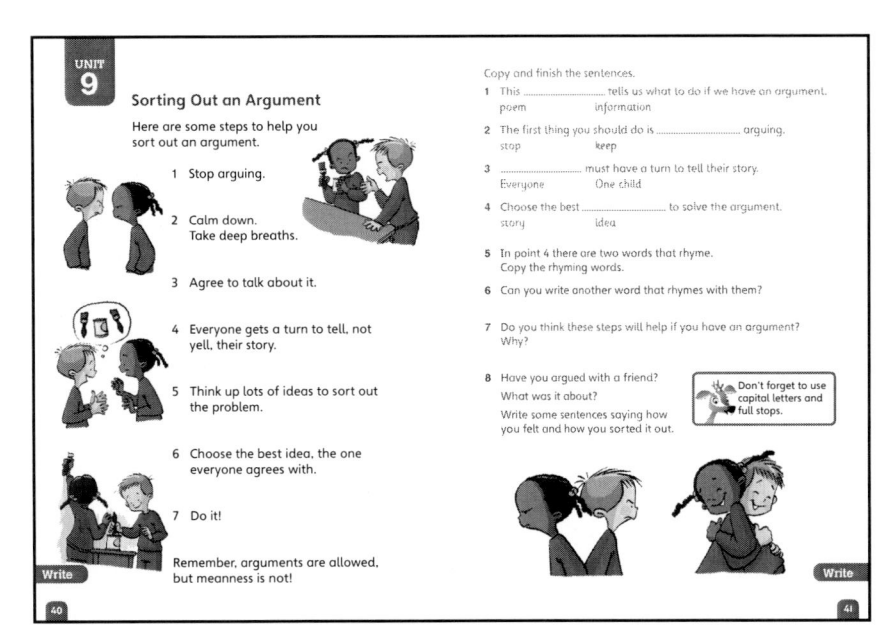

RESOURCE SHEET ANSWERS

Support

4. Everyone gets a turn to tell, not yell, their story.
2. Calm down. Take deep breaths.
6. Choose the best idea, the one everyone agrees with.
1. Stop arguing.
3. Agree to talk about it.
7. Do it!
5. Think up lots of ideas to sort out the problem.

Extension
Individual answers.

GOING DEEPER

- Encourage the children to share their ideas on how best to solve an argument.
- This unit could be a useful vehicle for children to express their anxieties about arguments over which they have little control, e.g. between other children when they have divided loyalties or between adults at home.
- Summarise the use of information texts. Brainstorm other times when they may be used.

BOOK 1   UNIT 10

UNIT FOCUS: Pattern and Rhyme

Investigating …
- reading and responding to poems that rhyme and have simple patterned stories
- how sounds, words and phrases are used and sequenced while looking at poems with a similar theme

TEACH/TALK

- Read the poem 'Birds in the Garden' to the children, either in groups or as a class.
- Discuss the pace and pattern of the poem.
- Encourage the children to imagine what they may smell, see, touch etc. if they were there.
- Read, discuss and ask the children to answer the questions.
- Discuss with the children what they like or dislike about the poem. Why?

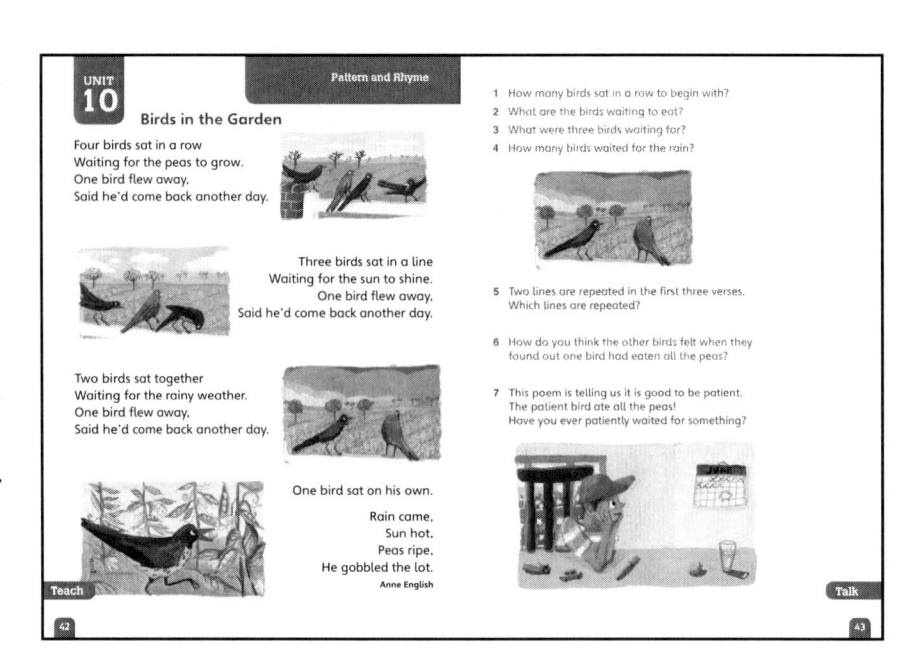

RESOURCES & ASSESSMENT BOOK

- **Support:** (vocabulary support) circle the rhyming words and fill in the gaps.
- **Extension:** answer questions and illustrate. Linked to Pupil Book Q7: *Have you ever patiently waited for something?*

PUPIL BOOK ANSWERS

1. Four birds.
2. The peas.
3. The sun to shine.
4. Two birds.
5. The following lines are repeated:
   One bird flew away,
   Said he'd come back another day.
6. Answer that suggests the children are able to empathise with the birds that didn't get any peas, e.g. hungry, grumpy, annoyed.
7. Individual answers.

RESOURCE SHEET ANSWERS

Support
Row rhymes with *grow*.
Line rhymes with *shine*.
Together rhymes with *weather*.
Away rhymes with *day*.
Hot rhymes with *lot*.

Extension
Individual answers.

GOING DEEPER

- Review the children's answers to the questions. Did they like the predictable pattern of the poem?
- Learn the poem by heart as a class, performing it to others with actions.
- Discuss in more detail the benefits of being patient.

BOOK 1 — UNIT 10

WRITE

- Encourage children to read the poem themselves or read the poem aloud to or with those who need support.
- Ask children to answer the questions individually.

RESOURCES & ASSESSMENT BOOK

- **Support:** (comprehension support) arrange pictures in the correct order.
- **Extension:** explain which poem they prefer. Linked to Pupil Book Q7: *Which poem do you like best? Why?* Encourage children to write simple sentences in response to this question.

PUPIL BOOK ANSWERS

1. The cow is chewing.
2. Quack
3. The dogs bark.
4. At the end of the poem.
5. black: quack, barked: sparked, stopped: hopped
6. Answer that suggests that because the cow kept chewing it wasn't worried about anything.
7. Individual answers.

RESOURCE SHEET ANSWERS

Support

1. picture with horse
2. picture with ducks
3. picture with dogs
4. picture with cats
5. picture with rabbits
6. picture of cow on its own

Extension

Individual answers.

GOING DEEPER

- Review children's answers to the questions.
- Discuss as a class which of the poems in Unit 10 children preferred and why. Encourage the children to give reasons for their preferences. They can discuss what they like and don't like about the poems.
- Read other nature poems to the children asking whether they like or dislike them and why.

BOOK 2

Book 2 Scope and Sequence

Unit	Unit Focus	Texts	Oxford Level	Oxford Reading Criterion Scale	Genre / text type
1	Familiar Settings	*Making Pancakes When My Mother Was Out*, Paddy Kinsale	10	standard 3, criteria 7, 20, 21, 23	fiction and settings
		A Present for Paul, Bernard Ashley	11		
2	Instructions	Make a Mess!	8	standard 3, criteria 6, 10, 20, 25, 26	instructions
		Making Butter	8		
3	Traditional Stories	*Little Red Riding Hood*	8	standard 3, criteria 7, 8, 9, 18, 20, 21, 22, 23	modern and traditional fairy tales
		Little Red Riding Hood, Heather Amery	8		
4	Explanations	*All About Me*	N/A	standard 3, criteria 8, 9, 10, 11, 18, 20, 25, 26, 29	non-fiction
		What Does My Heart Do? Brigid Avison	9		
5	Patterns on the Page	'Catch a Little Rhyme', Eve Merriam	9	standard 3, criteria 20, 21, 23	poetry
		'Leap Like a Leopard', John Foster	9		
6	Different Stories, Same Author	*The Gruffalo*, Julia Donaldson	9	standard 3, criteria 17, 20, 21, 23	different fiction stories by same author
		Monkey Puzzle, Julia Donaldson	9		
7	Finding Facts	Cats	9	standard 3, criteria 6, 10, 20, 24, 25, 26	non-fiction
		Pet Cat Facts	9		
8	Extended Stories	*Jellyfish Shoes*, Susan Gates	10	standard 3, criteria 7, 20, 21, 23	longer fiction stories
		'The Shoes Come Back!' from *Jellyfish Shoes*, Susan Gates	10		
9	Understanding Information Texts	Adventure World	9	standard 3, criteria 5, 6, 10, 20, 25, 26	non-fiction posters and planning
		Planning a Day Out	9		
10	Poetry	'I Wonder', Jeannie Kirby	8	standard 3, criteria 20, 21, 23	poetry
		'Ice Lolly', Pie Corbett	8		

BOOK 2

Resources & Assessment Book Support	Resources & Assessment Book Extension
completing sentences	predicting what happens next; describing and drawing
putting sentences into correct order	circling correct answers; writing about own experiences
putting pictures into correct order	making a list; writing instructions
circling the correct answer; writing explanations	writing instructions
describing characters	writing about what happens next
identifying true and false statements	comparing traditional tales
finding words in index and writing them in order	answering comprehension questions
matching words to their definition	researching information
cloze activity	answering questions and explaining opinions
cloze activity	completing a table and explaining opinions
describing the gruffalo	writing a book review
writing and ordering sentences	comparing stories
answering literal comprehension questions	adding further information
linking lines to complete sentences	writing about page layouts
putting sentences into correct order	answering questions with full sentences
writing about characters' feelings	predicting what happens next
underlining correct answers	explaining information
listing and writing about ideas	planning a day out
cloze activity	writing activity
looking more closely at the poem; answering questions	planning and writing a poem

BOOK 2   **UNIT 1**

UNIT FOCUS: Familiar Settings

Investigating ...
- the main characters, events and settings in familiar stories

TEACH/TALK

- Read the extract from *Making Pancakes When My Mother Was Out* to the children, either in groups or as a class.

- Discuss the following terms:

  Setting: Where does this part of the story take place?

  Character: Who is involved? Who are the main characters?

  Event: What happens?

- Highlight the fact that one of the children in the story is the narrator and his name is not known.

- Discuss and answer the questions with the class.

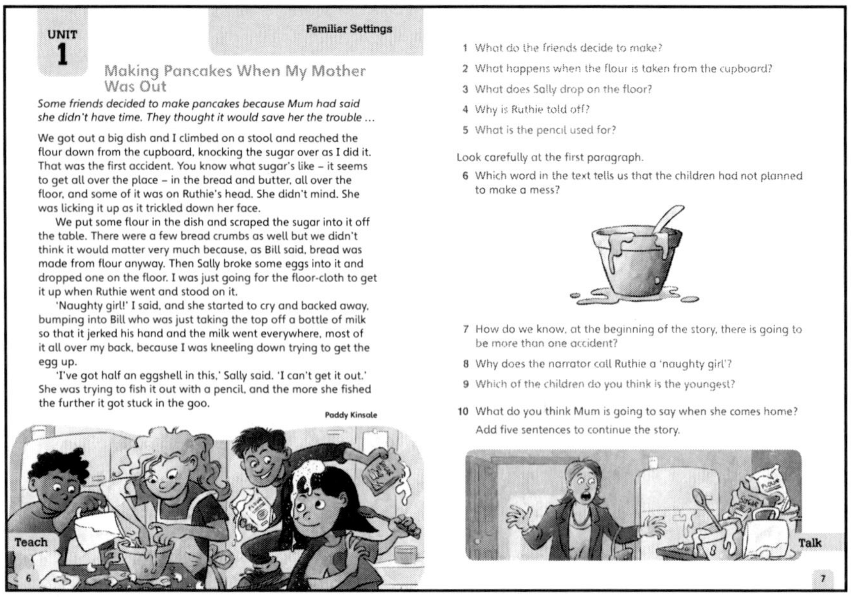

RESOURCES & ASSESSMENT BOOK

- **Support:** (comprehension support) complete the sentences.

- **Extension:** predicting what happens next; describe and draw a picture. Linked to Pupil Book Q10: *What do you think Mum is going to say when she comes home?* The children need to think about how Mum will react when she comes home. Will she laugh, scream, shout or cry? Discuss with the children how their mums may react.

PUPIL BOOK ANSWERS

1. Pancakes.
2. Sugar is spilt.
3. An egg.
4. She steps in the broken egg.
5. To try to get eggshell out of the pancake mixture.
6. The word 'accident'.
7. At the beginning of the extract it says 'That was the first accident' suggesting there are more to come!
8. Ruthie steps in the broken egg.
9. Answer that suggests why it is believed Ruthie is younger than the others, e.g. she doesn't say anything, she steps in the broken egg, she cries when she is told off.
10. Individual answers.

RESOURCE SHEET ANSWERS

Support

A
1. Sally broke some *eggs* into the bowl.
2. One egg was dropped on the *floor*.
3. *Ruthie* stood on the broken egg.
4. Ruthie bumped into *Bill*.
5. *Milk* went everywhere.

B. A floor-cloth was being used to clear up the broken egg up.

Extension
Individual answers.

GOING DEEPER

- As a class or group, review the children's answers to questions.

- Having discussed Mum's reaction, ask the children to read their versions of what happened when Mum comes home. Put the children in groups to act out their version of events.

- Discuss with the children whether they enjoyed the story. What did they like about it? What didn't they like about it?

40

BOOK 2 — UNIT 1

WRITE

- Ask the children to work in small groups or as individuals to look carefully at the extract.
- Ask the children to answer the questions individually. Remind the children that for the red questions they need to copy out the whole sentence.

RESOURCES & ASSESSMENT BOOK

- **Support:** (comprehension support) write sentences in the correct order and illustrate. Offer support reading the sentences if necessary. Children could work in pairs.
- **Extension:** circle the correct answers; write about their own experiences. Linked to Pupil Book Q8: *Have you ever been lost or felt very frightened?*

PUPIL BOOK ANSWERS

1. Pleasure is thinking about her baby brother Paul.
2. Pleasure had lost her dad.
3. He called her his big girl.
4. Answer that suggests that 'wiped off in a flash' means 'disappears quickly'.
5. Answer that suggests Pleasure's stomach did a 'head over heels' means it felt strange or gave a rolling feeling.
6. happy, pleased, bright, jolly
7. sad, worried, scared, upset, frightened, tearful
8. Individual answers.

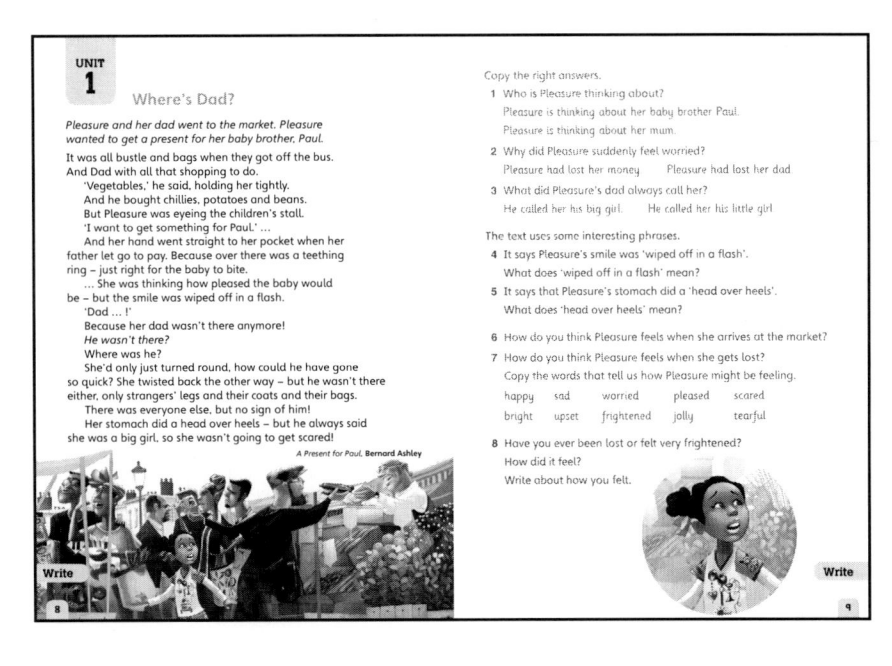

RESOURCE SHEET ANSWERS

Support

1. Pleasure and Dad go on the bus to the market.
2. Dad wants to buy some vegetables.
3. Pleasure sees a present for Paul.
4. Pleasure looks for her dad.
5. Pleasure isn't going to get scared.

A picture to show what they think happens next.

Extension

Where does the story take place? *the market*

Who is the main character? *Pleasure*

What happens? *Pleasure gets lost.*

Child's own sentences on a time when they have been lost or felt very frightened.

GOING DEEPER

- As a class or group, review the children's answers to questions.
- Having discussed with the class or group how they felt if they have ever been lost, use the opportunity to discuss what they should do if they were to get lost, for example, approach someone in uniform or a family with children, rather than a person on their own.
- Obtain a copy of the book *A Present for Paul* to read the ending of the story to the children.

BOOK 2 UNIT 2

UNIT FOCUS: Instructions

Investigating ...
- the role of instructions
- reading and following instructions
- layout of instructions

TEACH/TALK

- Give children a few simple instructions such as touch your nose, clap your hands. Gradually build up the number of instructions until they have four or five instructions. Write out the instructions in order.

- Discuss how they may be laid out, for example, using bullet points, numbers and so on. Be sure children understand what an instruction is.

- Highlight that instructions are given in an impersonal way. Discuss ways of writing instructions for different purposes, for example:
    - using the imperative mood, for example 'Sit down.'
    - using the auxiliary verb 'must', for example, 'You must sit down.'
    - using the second person present tense, for example, 'You sit down.'

- Look at the instructions for *Make a Mess!* Children discuss and answer the questions.

RESOURCES & ASSESSMENT BOOK

- **Support:** (comprehension support) numerically order the pictures.
- **Extension:** make a list. Linked to Pupil Book Q7: *Make a list of different things we need instructions for* and Q8: *Choose one thing you have listed and write what you would need to do it.* Children can do this resource sheet in pairs. Extend the activity by challenging children to write out the instructions for their chosen thing.

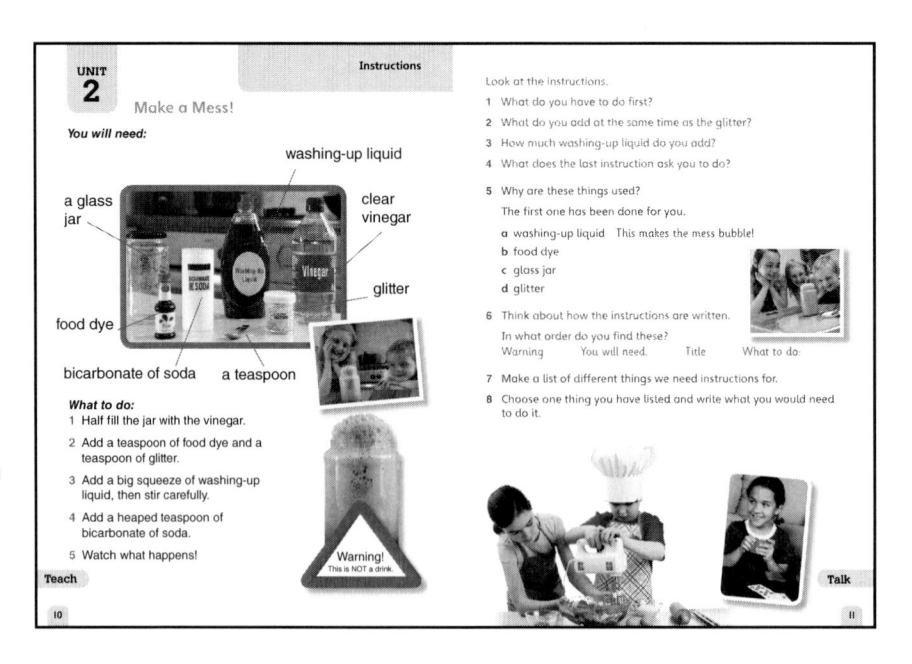

PUPIL BOOK ANSWERS

1. Fill the jar with the vinegar.
2. You add a teaspoon of food dye.
3. You need to add a big squeeze of washing-up liquid.
4. The last instruction asks you to watch what happens.
5. b food dye: to give the mess a colour
   c glass jar: to contain the ingredients of the mess
   d glitter: to give the mess a sparkle
6. Title, You will need:, What to do:, Warning
7. Child's own lists of different things instructions are needed for, e.g. putting together a toy and growing a seed.
8. Individual answers.

RESOURCE SHEET ANSWERS

Support

Picture 1 = 5

Picture 2 = 3

Picture 3 = 2

Picture 4 = 1

Picture 5 = 4

Extension

Individual answers.

GOING DEEPER

- Discuss children's answers to the questions.
- It is important the children can identify the different way instructions are written, for example, without the use of descriptive sentences.
- Follow the *Make a Mess!* instructions as a class. Discuss how they may be improved.

BOOK 2 — UNIT 2

WRITE

- Ask children to work in small groups or as individuals and look at the instructions for making butter.
- Ask children to answer the questions individually.

RESOURCES & ASSESSMENT BOOK

- **Support:** (comprehension support) circle the correct answer; write explanatory text.
- **Extension:** write their own instructions. Remind the children of the style of writing required for instructions. Linked to Pupil Book Q6: *How do you make a jam sandwich?*

PUPIL BOOK ANSWERS

1. Pour the cream into the jar and screw on the lid.
   Shake the jar for 20 minutes (or more), until you have big lumps in the cream.
   Put the paper towel in the sieve and place it over the bowl.
   Pour the contents from the jar into the sieve. The lumps are butter!
   Put your butter in the fridge.

2. four of: pour, screw, shake, put, place

3. To separate the lumps of butter from the cream.

4. Answer that suggests what the child thinks would be the hardest part of making the butter.

5. Answer that suggests that a clean jar with a lid needs to be used so that the butter can be eaten and the contents all stay in the jar while it is being shaken.

6. Child's own instructions on how to make a jam sandwich.

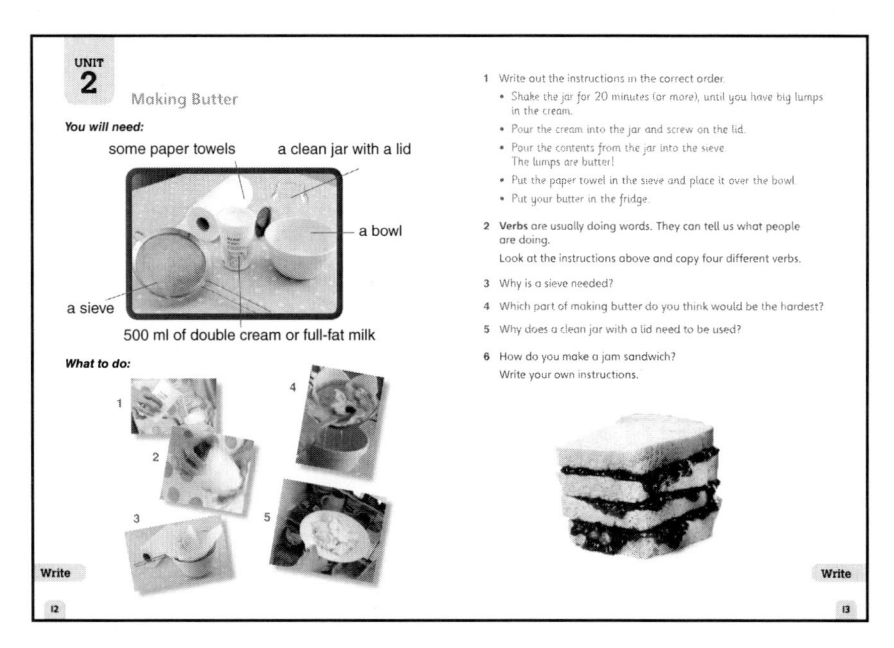

RESOURCE SHEET ANSWERS

Support
Correct answers circled:

1. cream
2. about 20 minutes
3. When there are lumps.
4. Answer written as sentence:
   The butter should be put in a fridge once it has been made to keep it cool and fresh.

Extension
Individual answers.

GOING DEEPER

- Review the children's answers. Compare the different ways children have written instructions for making a jam sandwich.
- Try making a jam sandwich according to the children's instructions.
- Put children in pairs and ask them to write short instructions for an activity of their choice.
- Create a 'Playground Games Instruction Manual'. Ask the children to try out the instructions to see if they work well.
- Encourage children to make butter according to the instructions. Ask them to comment on the instructions and whether they can be improved.
- Summarise the use of instructions. Brainstorm other times when they may be used.

BOOK 2

UNIT 3

UNIT FOCUS: Traditional Stories
Investigating ...
- alternative versions of traditional stories
- how 'good' and 'bad' characters are portrayed

TEACH/TALK

- After reading through the story, ask the children if they recognise it. Do they think it is the whole story? Introduce the voice of the story as the 'narrator'.
- Answer the questions with the children, encouraging empathy as the children discuss the characters.

RESOURCES & ASSESSMENT BOOK

- **Support:** (comprehension support) describing characters. Linked to Pupil Book Qs 5–8.
- **Extension:** finishing the story. Linked to Pupil Book Q10: *Finish this story.* Children are asked to draw pictures and write sentences about what they think happened next in pairs, small groups or as a class.

PUPIL BOOK ANSWERS

1. She always wore a red hooded top her granny gave her.
2. Some cakes and a drink.
3. In a field.
4. The wolf was hungry and wanted to see the cakes he could smell in Little Red Riding Hood's basket.
5. Little Red Riding Hood is a good character.
6. E.g. kind, thoughtful, happy, friendly
7. The wolf is a bad character.
8. E.g. sly, crafty, surprising, unfriendly
9. Answer that suggests the close relationship between Little Red Riding Hood and her granny, e.g. Granny gave Little Red Riding Hood the red top, Little Red Riding Hood wanted to take the fresh cakes to her Granny, Mum says how much Granny would like to see Little Red Riding Hood.
10. Individual answers.

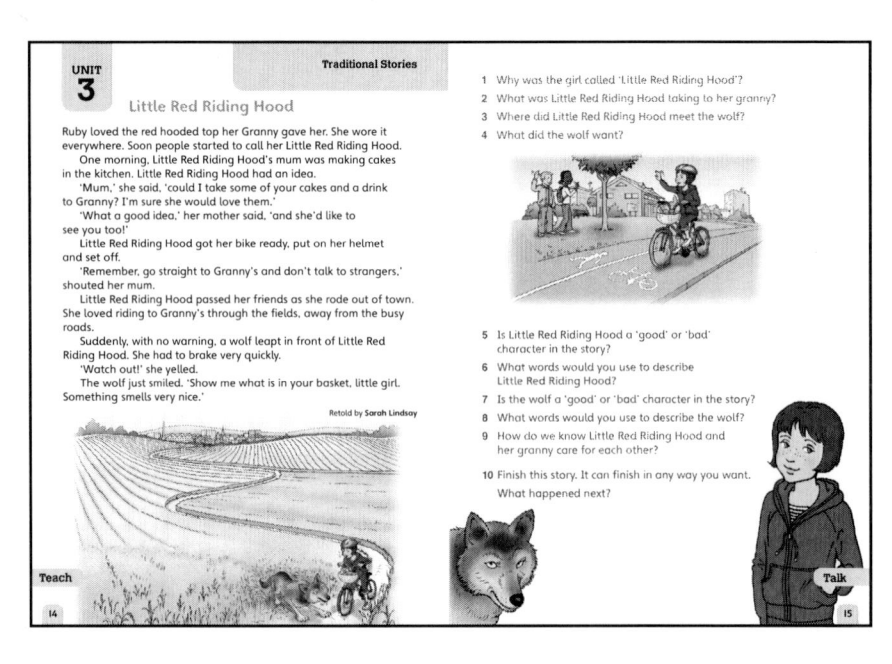

RESOURCE SHEET ANSWERS

Support

Little Red Riding Hood: e.g. kind, thoughtful, happy, friendly

Wolf: e.g. sly, crafty, surprising, unfriendly

Extension

Individual answers.

GOING DEEPER

- Review the children's answers to the questions. Encourage children to read aloud their own versions of what happened to Little Red Riding Hood and the wolf. Children can work in small groups to role-play the story.
- Discuss the more traditional version of the story.

BOOK 2 — UNIT 3

WRITE

- Explain to the children that this version of the story is simplified.
- Ask children to work as individuals or in small groups.

RESOURCES & ASSESSMENT BOOK

- **Support:** (comprehension support) true and false statements.
- **Extension:** comparing traditional tales. Linked to Pupil Book Q6a: *List what is different about the two stories* and Q6b: *List what is the same about the two stories.* Encourage children to write specific information relating back to the original texts. It may be useful for children to have access to the first story as well as the second.

PUPIL BOOK ANSWERS

1. Granny made Little Red Riding Hood's *cloak*.
2. Little Red Riding Hood's granny felt *unwell*.
3. Little Red Riding Hood walked through the *forest*.
4. Little Red Riding Hood was scared of the *wolf*.
5. the forest: big, dark
   the cloak: bright red
   the wolf: big, black
6. a The differences between the two stories: e.g. Little Red Riding Hood was on a bike in the first but walking in the second, Granny was well in the first story but unwell in the second.
   b The similarities between the two stories: e.g. Little Red Riding Hood was the name of the girl in both stories, Little Red Riding Hood was met by a wolf in both stories.
7. Individual answers.

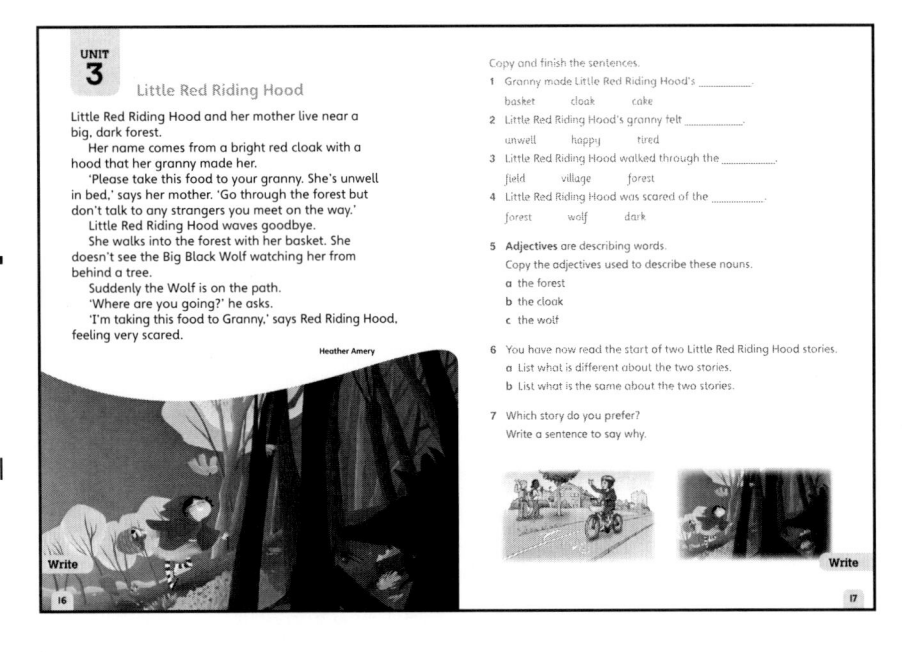

RESOURCE SHEET ANSWERS

Support

1. false
2. false
3. true
4. true
5. false
6. false
7. false

Extension
Individual answers.

GOING DEEPER

- Review the children's answers to the questions.
- In larger groups, find out which version of the story was more popular by asking children to stand in two groups.
- In small groups, the children can be encouraged to re-enact one of the versions of the *Little Red Riding Hood* story.
- To compare another version of the Little Red Riding story, read *Little Fred Riding Hood* by Michael Cox.
- Look at other traditional stories. Draw the children's attention to 'good' or 'bad' characters (heroes and villains) in, for example, *Cinderella* or *Snow White*.

BOOK 2 — UNIT 4

UNIT FOCUS: Explanations
Investigating …
- explanation texts
- how non-fiction material can be presented

TEACH/TALK

- Have a range of non-fiction texts for the children to look at. Spend time discussing the front covers, indexes and glossaries. Where are they found in the books? What are they used for?
- With the children, look at the front cover and index so the children can discuss them as a group or class.
- Answer the questions.

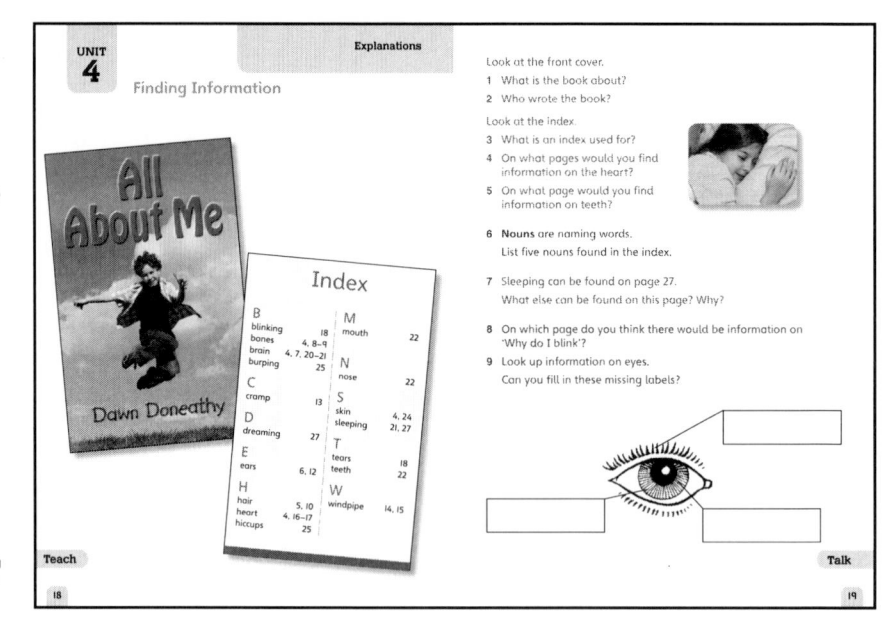

RESOURCES & ASSESSMENT BOOK

- **Support:** (comprehension support) find words in the index, write them in order.
- **Extension:** answer the comprehension questions. Linked to Pupil Book Q9: *Look up information on eyes.*

PUPIL BOOK ANSWERS

1. The book is about the body.
2. Dawn Doneathy.
3. To direct the reader to a particular page for information on a particular subject.
4. You would find information on the heart on pages 4, 16–17.
5. You would find information on teeth on page 22.
6. Five nouns listed from the index, e.g. bones, brain, cramp, ears, hair, heart, hiccups, mouth, nose, skin, tears, teeth, windpipe.
7. Dreaming can also be found on page 27 because it happens when you sleep.
8. On page 18 it is likely you would find information on 'Why do I blink?'.
9. [labelled eye diagram: eyelashes, iris, pupil]

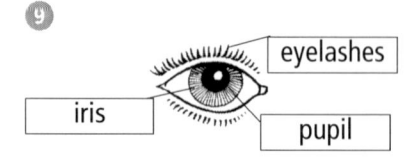

RESOURCE SHEET ANSWERS

Support
1st cramp p. 13
2nd blinking p. 18
3rd mouth p. 22
4th burping p. 25
    hiccups p. 25
5th dreaming p. 27

Extension
[labelled eye diagram: eyelashes, iris, pupil]

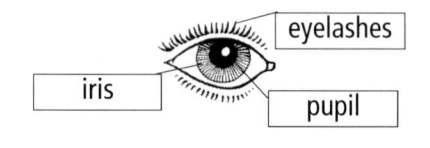

1. Blinking stops the eyes from feeling dry and sore.
2. We blink thousands of times a day.
3. Eyelashes help stop dust and grit getting into our eyes.

GOING DEEPER

- As a class or group, review the children's answers to the questions.
- It is important the children can identify the different ways information can be passed on to other people. As a class make a list of all the different ways we now receive information. Discuss which ways the children find the most informative.

BOOK 2 — UNIT 4

WRITE

- Ask the children to work as individuals or in small groups and read the information.
- Ask them to answer the questions individually or in small groups.
- Introduce the term 'glossary' to the children. Show them examples in books and highlight how it is laid out, e.g. alphabetically, and what it is used for.

RESOURCES & ASSESSMENT BOOK

- **Support:** (comprehension support) complete a glossary by matching the body part to its definition.
- **Extension:** find information about a body part. Linked to Pupil Book Q7: *Choose a part of your body. Find out about it.* Children can work in pairs or individually.

PUPIL BOOK ANSWERS

1. The heart is a *muscle*.
2. The heart pumps *blood* around your body.
3. The heart makes *two* sounds close together.
4. Your heart is a bit *bigger* than your fist.
5. a The child's choice of five words that could go in a glossary.
   b The five words from Q5a written in alphabetical order.
6. Individual answers.
7. Child's own investigation into a part of the body.

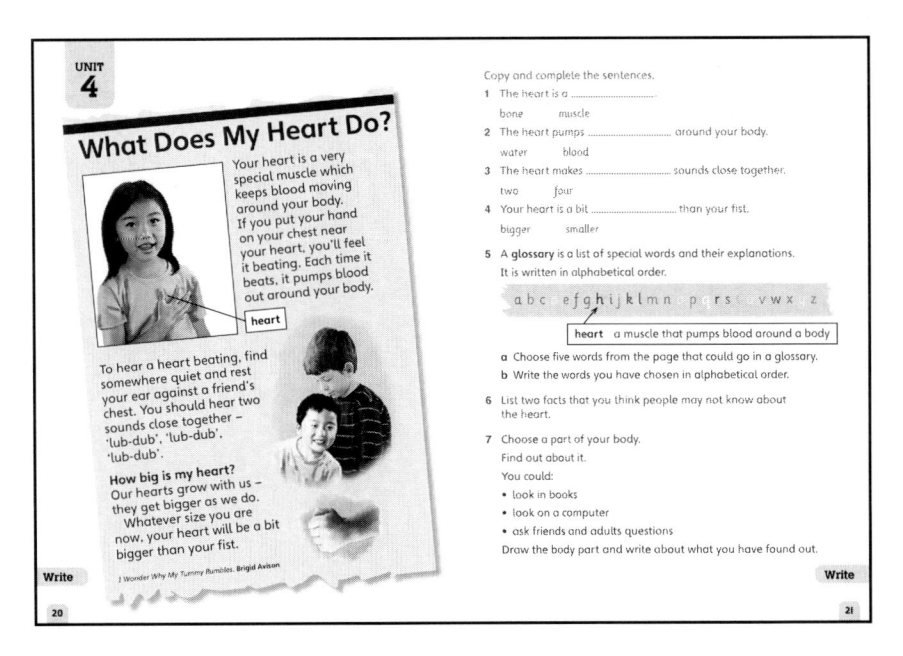

RESOURCE SHEET ANSWERS

Support

blood: the red liquid the heart pumps around your body

chest: the upper part of the front of your body, between the waist and the neck

fist: your hand when the fingers are tightly tucked into the palm

heart: the part of your body that pumps blood around it

muscle: something in your body that tightens and loosens to help your body move

Extension

Individual answers.

GOING DEEPER

- As a class or in groups review the children's answers. Review how the structure of a non-fiction text makes it easier to access information.
- Ask the children to work in pairs or small groups and prepare a presentation for the rest of the class, following question 7. Encourage them to listen to one another's ideas and present the information in as interesting a way as possible.

BOOK 2

UNIT 5

UNIT FOCUS: Patterns on the Page

Investigating ...
- reading and responding to poems that focus on the playful exploration of language
- the structure and language patterns of poems

TEACH/TALK

- Read the poem 'Catch a Little Rhyme' to children, either in groups or as a class.
- Encourage children to join in, following the rhythm and keeping time.
- Discuss the poem and answer the questions.

RESOURCES & ASSESSMENT BOOK

- **Support:** (comprehension support) insert the missing words.
- **Extension:** answer questions and explain opinions. Linked to Pupil Book Q7a: *Do you like the poem?*

PUPIL BOOK ANSWERS

1. The rhyme ran right out the door.
2. The rhyme was in a hat when it turned into a cat.
3. The rhyme stretched into a whale.
4. The rhyme had been fed tin and paper when it turned into a skyscraper.
5. boat: goat,
   time: rhyme,
   bicycle: icicle,
   floor: door,
   kite: sight,
   tail: whale
6. Answer that makes reference to how the person catching the rhyme may be feeling, e.g. frustrated and exhausted.
7. a Answer reflecting whether the child likes the poem and why.
   b Answer stating if the poem makes the child smile and why.

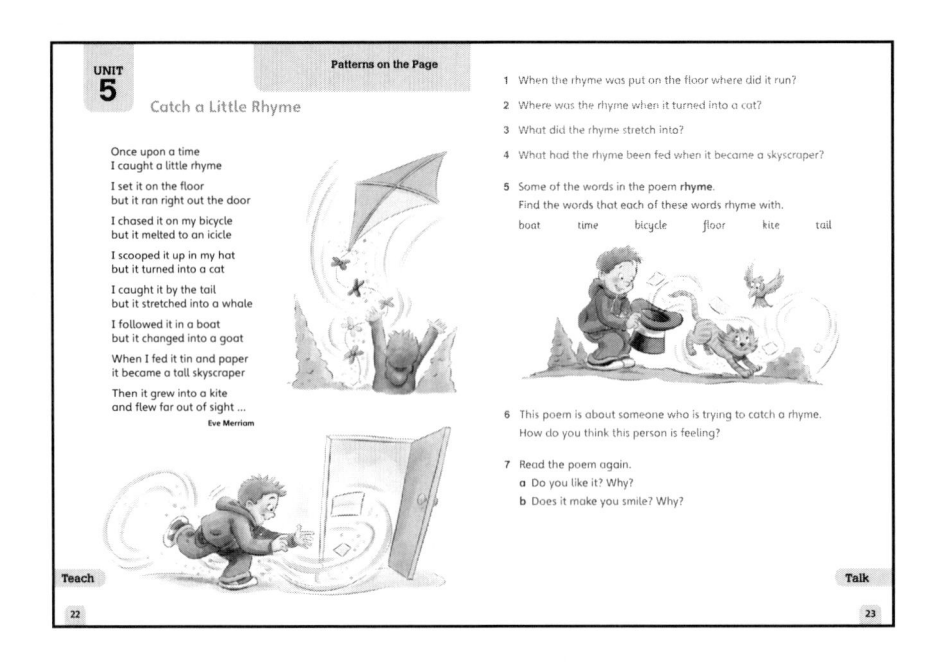

RESOURCE SHEET ANSWERS

Support
rhyme
door
icicle
cat
whale
goat
skyscraper
sight

Extension
Individual answers.

GOING DEEPER

- As a class or in groups, review children's answers to the questions.
- Ask the children to work in groups or pairs and think of actions to go with the poem. Children can look at the artwork for ideas but should also come up with their own ideas. Encourage children to perform the poem with their actions to the rest of the class.

BOOK 2 UNIT 5

WRITE

- Ask children to read the poem in small groups or as individuals.
- Children answer the questions individually.

RESOURCES & ASSESSMENT BOOK

- **Support:** (comprehension support) fill the gaps.
- **Extension:** complete the table, explain their choices. Linked to Pupil Book Q10b: *Which poem do you prefer?*

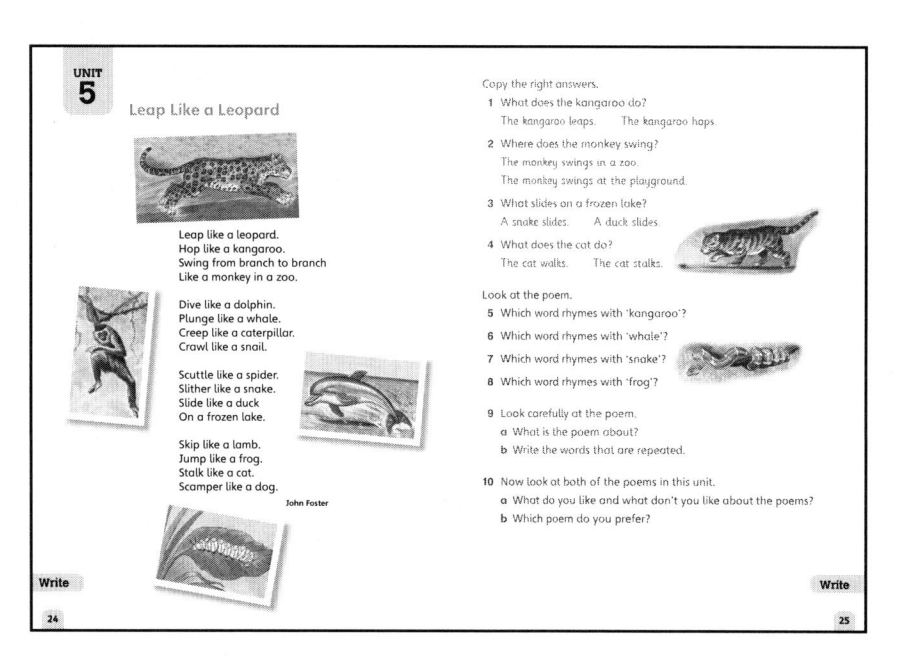

PUPIL BOOK ANSWERS

1. The kangaroo hops.
2. The monkey swings in a zoo.
3. A duck slides.
4. The cat stalks.
5. The word 'zoo' rhymes with 'kangaroo'.
6. The word 'snail' rhymes with 'whale'.
7. The word 'lake' rhymes with 'snake'.
8. The word 'dog' rhymes with 'frog'.
9. a An answer that suggests the poem describes the way animals move.
   b Answer that states the words 'like a' are repeated throughout the poem.
10. a Answer that suggests the child has made a specific choice between the two poems and is able to comment on what they like or don't like in each one.
    b An answer that states which of the two poems they prefer.

RESOURCE SHEET ANSWERS

Support
Two further verses of 'Leap Like a Leopard' are given with some words removed. The children are asked to add their own words.
It doesn't matter if they aren't correct words; the emphasis is on continuing the pattern. The first two gaps should be verbs; the third should rhyme with 'bear'. The fourth and fifth gaps should also be verbs, and the sixth gap should rhyme with 'high'.

Extension
Individual answers.

GOING DEEPER

- As a class or group, review the children's answers. Ask the children to invent actions for the poem, which can then be performed.
- Encourage children to read aloud their version of two verses from the poem.
- Discuss the children's thoughts on the two poems. Which poem did they like best and why?

BOOK 2 UNIT 6

UNIT FOCUS: Different Stories, Same Author
Investigating ...
- children's understanding of characters, settings and events
- how characters, settings and events vary in stories written by the same author

TEACH/TALK

- Read the extract from *The Gruffalo* to the class.
- You may like to recap the terms **character**, **setting** and **event**.
- Answer the questions as a class or in small groups.

RESOURCES & ASSESSMENT BOOK

- **Support:** (vocabulary support) describe the gruffalo.
- **Extension:** book review. Linked to Pupil Book Q9: *Now write a book review of a book you enjoy.*

PUPIL BOOK ANSWERS

1. Through the deep dark wood.
2. A fox.
3. His underground house.
4. The gruffalo has 'terrible tusks, and terrible claws, And terrible teeth in terrible jaws.'
5. Clever: the mouse tricks the fox into not eating him;
   brave: the mouse doesn't appear scared of the fox;
   brown: the fox describes the mouse as 'brown'.
6. Answer giving more adjectives that may describe the mouse.
7. Answer stating what the child likes about the story.
8. Answer stating what the child doesn't like about the story.
9. A book review of the child's choice that includes the title, the author's name, where the story is set, what happens, who the main characters are and why their friends should read it.

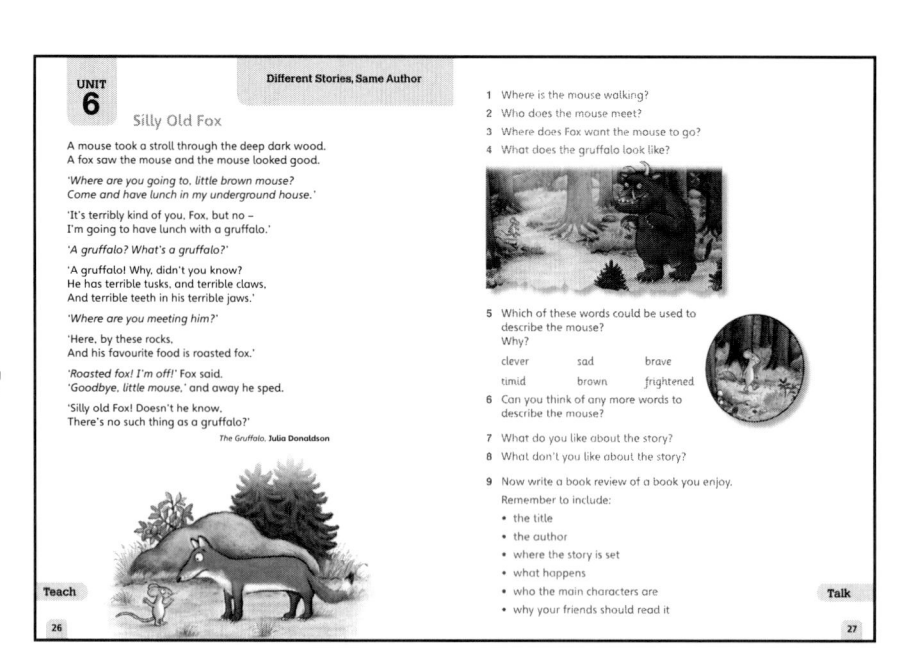

RESOURCE SHEET ANSWERS

Support
The child is asked to write as many descriptive words as they can about the gruffalo. They then need to use some of these words in a sentence describing the gruffalo.

Extension
This resource sheet gives an outline that the children can use when writing the book review.

GOING DEEPER

- Review children's answers to the questions. Encourage them to explain why they came up with the answers they did. What evidence did they find in the extract or pictures?
- Use hot-seating as a tool to explore the characters.
- Obtain a copy of the book *The Gruffalo* and read the whole story to the children. Discuss whether their opinions of the story have changed. In groups, encourage children to act out the story and perform it to the rest of the class.
- Ask children to write the character of the mouse into a story of their own.

BOOK 2 — UNIT 6

WRITE

- Ask children to read the extract from *Monkey Puzzle* as individuals or in small groups.
- Ask the children to answer the questions individually.

RESOURCES & ASSESSMENT BOOK

- **Support:** (comprehension support) write and order the sentences.
- **Extension:** story comparison. Linked to Pupil Book Q6a: *Write a list of the things that are similar in both stories* and Q6b: *Write a list of the things that are different in both stories.* Children can work in pairs or individually.

PUPIL BOOK ANSWERS

1. Monkey has lost his mum.
2. The butterfly helped the monkey.
3. The elephant is described as having baggy knees.
4. No.
5. Clues given about the monkey's mum: she is big, her tail coils round trees, she has more legs than a snake!
6. a Answer stating what the child found similar about the two stories.
   b Answer stating what the child found different about the two stories.
7. Answer stating which story the child enjoyed the most and why.

RESOURCE SHEET ANSWERS

Support

1. 'I've lost my mum!'
2. 'I'll help you find her,' said Butterfly.
3. 'No, no, no! That's an elephant.'
4. 'No, no, no! That's a snake.'
5. 'It's legs we're looking for now, you say?'

Extension
Individual answers.

GOING DEEPER

- Review children's answers to the questions.
- Encourage children to role-play the story, repeating the key elements of the repetitive language used.
- Obtain a copy of *Monkey Puzzle* and read the whole story to children. Discuss whether their opinions of the story have changed.
- Challenge children to find out more about Julia Donaldson. Her website, www.juliadonaldson.co.uk, has information for the children to explore.

BOOK 2   UNIT 7

UNIT FOCUS: Finding Facts
Investigating ...
- non-fiction texts
- information texts with different layouts

TEACH/TALK

- Discuss with the children how the information text is organised.
  - The bullet points detail general points on cats.
  - Information is given under sub-headings to make reference easier.
- Read through the text. Encourage children to discuss and answer the questions.
- Q5: Some children may need support with this question. They could be given the three definitions and asked to match them to the correct words. More confident children could identify words that they are unsure of and look them up in a dictionary. Children may find that the words 'pride' and 'relax' have more than one definition. These are homonyms.

RESOURCES & ASSESSMENT BOOK

- **Support:** (comprehension support) answer the questions.
- **Extension:** add further information to the sections. Linked to Pupil Book Q7a: *Write one or two of your own sentences to add to each section.*

PUPIL BOOK ANSWERS

1. Yes
2. They relax in water.
3. Tigers
4. Meat

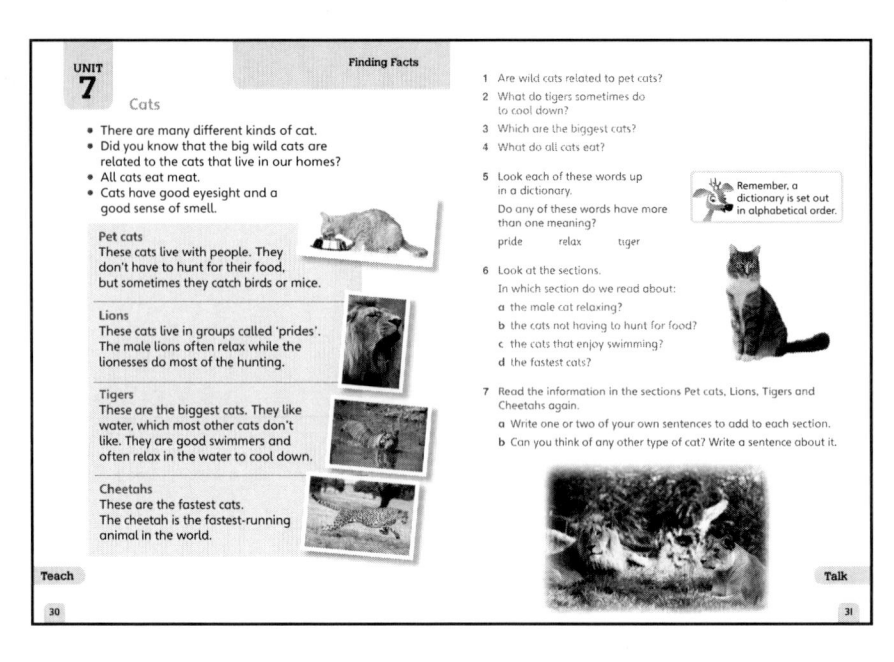

5. pride: a group of lions that live together
   relax: to feel calm and enjoy free time
   tiger: a large wild cat with black and orange stripes
   Pride and relax have more than one meaning.

6. a Lions.
   b Pet cats.
   c Tigers.
   d Cheetahs.

7. Children are required to find more information to add to each section on Pet cats, Lions, Tigers and Cheetahs, and a sentence on another type of cat.

RESOURCE SHEET ANSWERS

Support

1. chase
2. cheese
3. cat, cheetah
4. cave

5. chess

The children are asked to look at a dictionary page to find the words that answer the questions.

Extension

The child is required to add further information to the sections on Pet cats, Lions, Tigers and Cheetahs. Encourage children to source information from carefully selected books.

GOING DEEPER

- As a class or group, work through the children's answers to the questions.
- It is important the children can discuss the layout of this information text and distinguish why information texts are set out in such a way.
- Ask the children what else may be added to this page, and encourage them to share their ideas.
- Discuss homonyms with the children. Can they think of any other examples?

BOOK 2 — UNIT 7

WRITE

- Encourage the children, individually or in small groups, to look carefully at the pictures and text in order to extract all the relevant information needed.

RESOURCES & ASSESSMENT BOOK

- **Support:** (comprehension support) linking lines to complete sentences.
- **Extension:** write about page layout. Linked to Pupil Book Q8: *Look at the information on 'Cats' on page 30 and 'Cat facts' on page 32 again. Write a sentence saying which is set out in the most helpful way.*

PUPIL BOOK ANSWERS

1. Every day a cat will wash itself for *hours*.
2. If a cat *purrs* it is happy.
3. Cats scratch to exercise their muscles.
4. Most cats like being brushed.
5. Kittens learn to hunt while they are playing.
6. attention: to take notice
   muscle: a band of tissue in a body that moves
   hair ball: a ball of hair
7. Answer that suggests that most cats like being brushed as it mimics the cat washing itself, or that it likes the feeling of being brushed.
8. A sentence stating which information is set out in the most useful way and why.

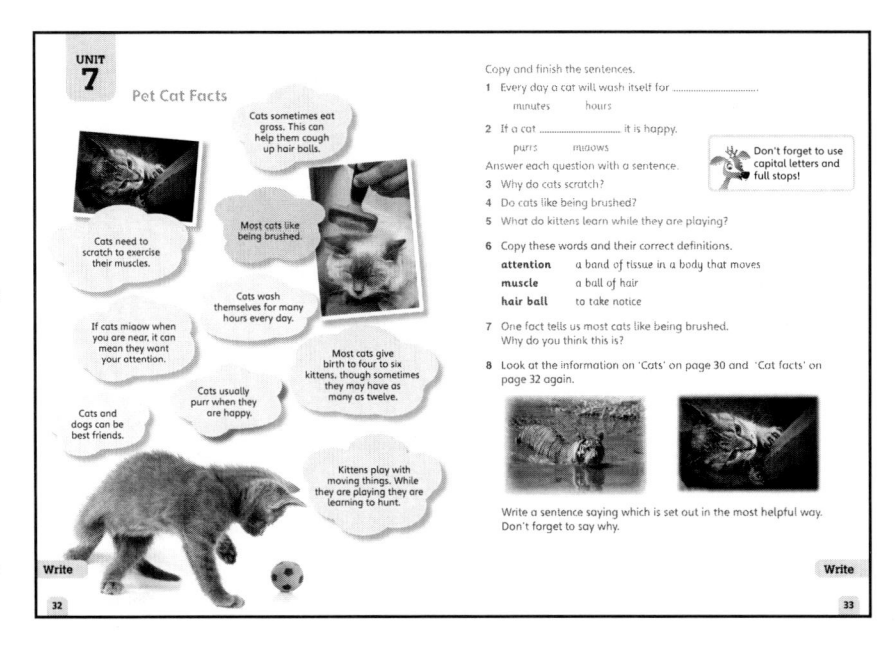

RESOURCE SHEET ANSWERS

Support

A
1. Most cats like being brushed.
2. Cats sometimes eat grass.
3. Cats wash themselves for many hours every day.
4. Cats usually purr when they are happy.
5. Cats and dogs can be best friends.
6. Most cats give birth to four to six kittens.
7. Kittens play with moving things.
8. If cats miaow when you are near, it can mean they want your attention.
9. Cats need to scratch to exercise their muscles.

B Answer stating which fact the child finds most interesting.

Extension

Questions in this resource sheet help the children look in more detail at the layout of the two pieces of information in this unit and ask them to be specific about which they prefer.

GOING DEEPER

- Review children's answers to the questions.
- Summarise when and how the children may use information texts.
- Children could add further information to one of the cat texts. Where would they look for further information? How would they take notes?

53

BOOK 2 UNIT 8

UNIT FOCUS: Extended Stories
Investigating ...
- exploring a longer story
- summarising a plot and making links between events
- what speech might tell us about a character
- predicting what might happen

TEACH/TALK

- Read the extract from *Jellyfish Shoes* to the children, either as a class or in groups.
- Discuss the following terms:

Setting: Where does this part of the story take place?
Character: Who is involved? Who is/are the main character(s)?
Event: What happens?

- Take time to help the children recognise the key events in the story so far.

Discuss with the children how notes can be made about the extract, e.g. where details can be left out to just provide the skeleton of what happened in a few words.

- Encourage the children to discuss and answer the questions.

RESOURCES & ASSESSMENT BOOK

- **Support:** (comprehension support) write the sentences in the correct order.
- **Extension:** answer the questions.
  Linked to Pupil Book Q8–9: *Are you enjoying the story so far? Is there a line which makes you want to read more of the story?*

PUPIL BOOK ANSWERS

1. Yes, Laura liked her new jelly shoes at the beginning of the story.
2. Scott is Laura's brother.
3. Laura does not like jellyfish as they are messy and remind her of cow-pats.
4. Laura threw her shoes in the sea because Scott said they were made from jellyfish.
5. pink, see-through
6. the jellyfish
7. e.g. – Laura steps on a jellyfish.
   – Scott tells her how jelly shoes are made.
   – Laura throws her shoes in the sea.
8. Answer stating whether the child is enjoying the story so far and why.
9. Answer highlighting a line in the story that makes the child want to read more.

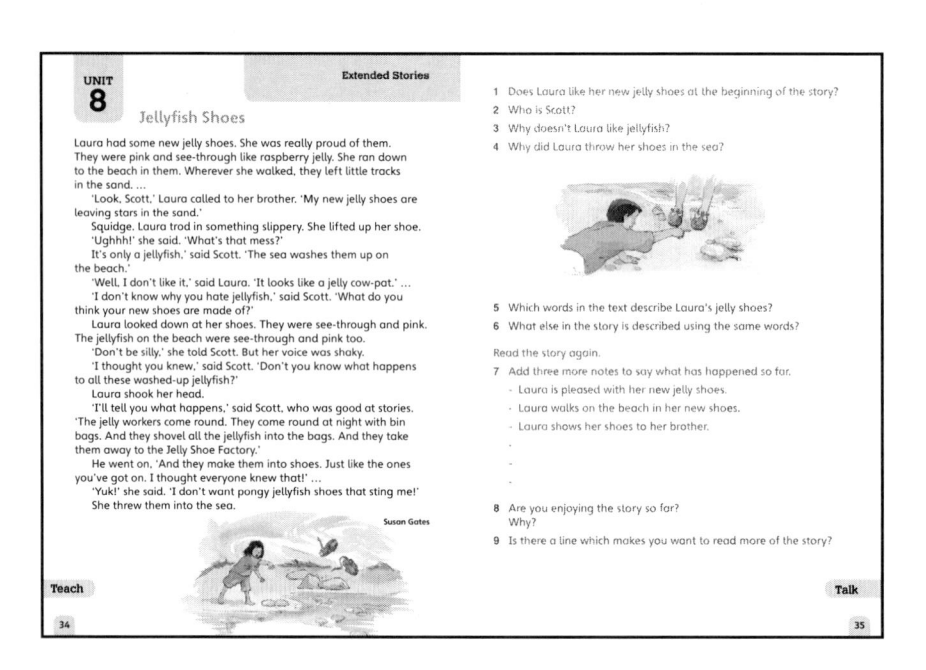

RESOURCE SHEET ANSWERS

Support

Laura is proud of her new jelly shoes.

Laura stands on a jellyfish.

Scott tells Laura about the jelly workers.

Laura does not like her jellyfish shoes.

Laura throws her shoes in the sea.

Extension

Questions that explore what the children feel about the story so far. Individual answers.

GOING DEEPER

- Review the children's answers to the questions. Encourage them to explain why they came up with the answers they did – what evidence did they find in the extract or pictures?
- Encourage the children to think how they might react if they were told of the jelly workers described in the story. Hot-seating could be used for this.

54

BOOK 2   UNIT 8

WRITE

- Introduce this extract as a continuation of *Jellyfish Shoes*.
- Where possible, this extract is intended to be used for individual or small group work.

RESOURCES & ASSESSMENT BOOK

- **Support:** (comprehension support) write about the main character's feelings.
- **Extension:** predict what might happen next. Linked to Pupil Book Q8–9: *What do you think Scott says? How does Laura react to what Scott says?*

PUPIL BOOK ANSWERS

1. Laura had a *bad* dream.
2. That night the *jellyfish* shoes were washed up on the beach.
3. Mum found Laura's jelly shoes.
4. Laura did not want her jelly shoes back because she thought they were made of jellyfish.
5. rushed
6. puzzled
7. Scott looked guilty because the story he told Laura was why she did not like her shoes anymore.
8. Answer that suggests what is thought Scott says next to Laura.
9. Answer that suggests how Laura reacts to what Scott now says to her.

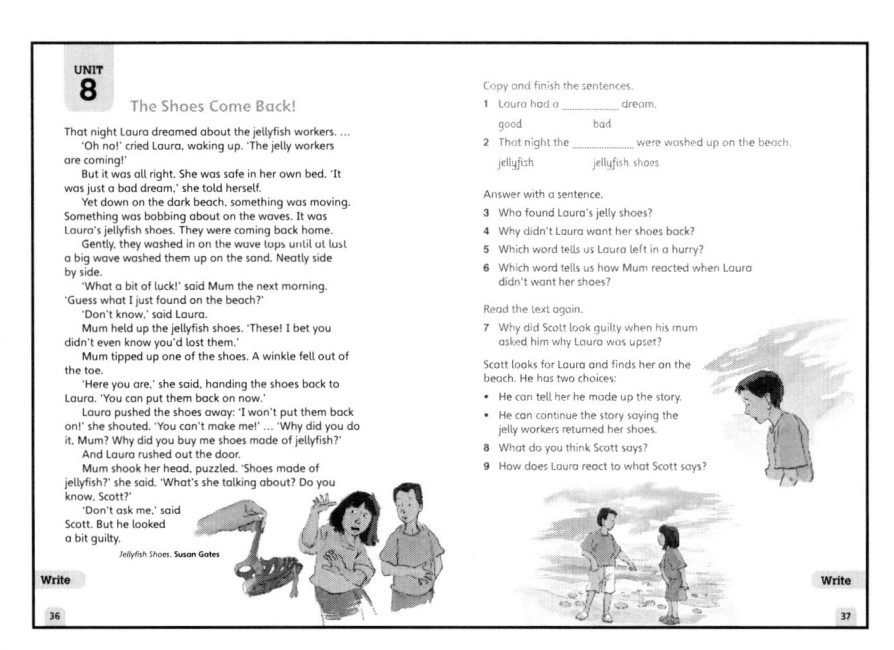

RESOURCE SHEET ANSWERS

Support

The children are asked to write as many descriptive words as they can about how Laura feels, e.g. frightened, upset, terrified. They then need to use some of these words in a sentence to describe how Laura feels and why she feels like this.

Extension

This gives a structure on which to write about the choice they think Scott made and what they then think happens next.

GOING DEEPER

- As a class review the children's answers to the questions.
- Encourage the children to discuss whether they are enjoying the story so far. Why?
- Discuss techniques used by the author that help to sustain the reader's interest.
- Obtain a copy of *Jellyfish Shoes* to continue reading the story so the children can discover how the story concludes.

BOOK 2
UNIT 9

UNIT FOCUS: Understanding Information Texts

Investigating ...
- information texts
- questioning and evaluating the usefulness of information texts

TEACH/TALK

- Discuss adventure playgrounds with the children. Encourage them to share their experiences.
- Show children the adventure playground leaflet. Ask for children's initial reactions. Do they like its layout, the colours used and so on?
- Look at the leaflet in more detail, either as a class or in groups. Children answer the questions.

RESOURCES & ASSESSMENT BOOK

- **Support:** (comprehension support) underline the correct answers.
- **Extension:** explaining the information. Linked to Pupil Book Q9: *Why are each of these bits of information important?*

PUPIL BOOK ANSWERS

1. An adventure playground called Adventure World.
2. £5.00.
3. Play in a pirate ship, go on the trampoline and swingboats, and play in tree houses, sandpits and on a soft play island.
4. No, you don't need a packed lunch as the café sells food.
5. Three words e.g. fun, fantastic, best
6. Yes.
7. The pirate ship and the soft play island.
8. To encourage other children to want to go to the playground. They may think it would be great to make their brother walk the plank!

9. | What you can do there | This tells you what you could visit. |
   |---|---|
   | Cost | This tells you how much it will cost. |
   | Opening times | This tells you when it is open. |
   | Comments from people who have already visited | This tells you what others thought about their visit. |

RESOURCE SHEET ANSWERS

Support

1. Yes.
2. He talks about his brother.
3. He said he made his brother walk the plank.
4. Answer that suggests that Tuhil would like to return to the Adventure Park as he had so much fun on his first visit.

Extension

This resource sheet helps the child evaluate the information the leaflet provides.

GOING DEEPER

- Review children's answers to the questions.
- Draw attention to the alliteration used in the leaflet. Ask children to find other examples, such as 'terrific trampolining'. Ask children to think of a place they have visited and use alliteration to describe it.
- Show children other leaflets advertising places. Look at what they all have in common.

BOOK 2

UNIT 9

WRITE

- Ask children to work individually or in small groups, and answer the questions.

RESOURCES & ASSESSMENT BOOK

- **Support:** (comprehension support) list ideas, write about one.
- **Extension:** plan a day out. Linked to Pupil Book Q10: *Look at the 'What shall we take?' section. Write in note form what you need to take.*

PUPIL BOOK ANSWERS

1. There are many *exciting* places to visit.
2. Sometimes it is cheaper to buy a *family* ticket.
3. *Websites* often have a map to show how to get to a place.
4. On a long day out think about taking some *snacks*.
5. seaside
6. cheaper
7. Answer stating which days out the child would enjoy and why.
8. Answer stating three things the child may spend his/her money on, e.g. souvenirs, sweets, postcard.
9. Answer that suggests which are the most appropriate clothes for the day out the child has chosen and why, e.g. weather, indoors/outdoors, activity.
10. Answer listing items the child would need to take with them.

RESOURCE SHEET ANSWERS

Support
Suggestions are made on different days out the children may have been on. The children are then asked to choose the day they enjoyed the most and state why.

Extension
Answers that show plans that refer to the information in the 'Planning a day out' spread in the Pupil Book, and lists of things to take that are as detailed as possible.

GOING DEEPER

- Review children's answers to the questions.
- Compare the children's lists of what to take on a day out.
- Discuss as a class what the most popular type of day out is. Why do they think this is the case?

BOOK 2 — UNIT 10

UNIT FOCUS: Poetry

Investigating ...
- responding to poems that focus closely on things
- the recall of personal experience
- the way sounds, words and phrases are used and sequenced
- links to the children's senses, building on work previously done in Year 1

TEACH/TALK

- Introduce both poems for this unit, explaining that they are both about 'really looking' at things. The first poem is a more general look at why things are the way they are, while the second poem takes a closer look at what happens when you eat an ice lolly.
- Read the poem 'I Wonder' to the children, either in groups or as a class.
- Children discuss the poem as a class, in small groups or pairs. They answer the questions.

RESOURCES & ASSESSMENT BOOK

- **Support:** (comprehension support) fill in the gaps.
- **Extension:** write about the poem. Linked to Pupil Book Q7: *Do you like this poem? Why?*

PUPIL BOOK ANSWERS

1. Why is the grass *green*?
2. Why is the moon *not quite round*?
3. Who lights the *stars*?
4. Who paints the *rainbow in the sky*?
5. Nest rhymes with rest;
   green rhymes with seen;
   round rhymes with found;
   suppose rhymes with knows;
   sky rhymes with high;
   out rhymes with about.
6. Answer that suggests whether the children think Dad actually knows the answer to all the questions. The reason Dad won't answer her questions is because he doesn't know the answers!
7. Answer that states whether the child likes the poem and why.
8. Answer that states the child's favourite line, if they have one.

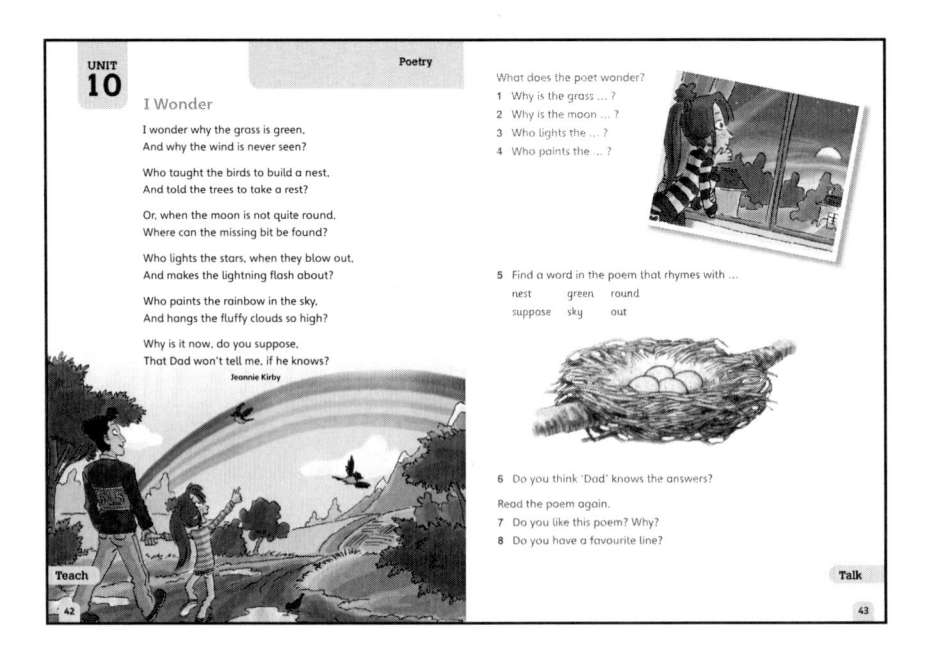

RESOURCE SHEET ANSWERS

Support
Gaps filled in the following order:
seen, rest, found, about,
high, knows.

Extension
This resource sheet is designed as an aid in recording the child's thoughts on the first poem, but can be used for children to evaluate any poem.

GOING DEEPER

- Review the children's answers to the questions.
- Discuss the pace of the poem and the fact it has a slightly dreamy quality to it. Ask children to share their thoughts on what they wonder about.
- Children could work in groups to learn the poem and perform it to an audience.

BOOK 2 — UNIT 10

WRITE

- Ask the children to read this poem to themselves. Read the poem aloud to or with children who need support.
- Ask them what the poem is 'really looking' at.
- Ask children to answer the questions.

RESOURCES & ASSESSMENT BOOK

- **Support:** (comprehension support) a closer look at the poem; answer the questions. Linked to Pupil Book Qs 3–5.
- **Extension:** plan and write a poem. Linked to Pupil Book Q8: *Think of something else that is messy to eat.* Encourage the children to imagine eating it. How do they eat it? How messy does it make them? How do they stop themselves from getting messy? Link the food to the five senses.

PUPIL BOOK ANSWERS

1. A red rocket is a lolly.
2. The poem says to lick the lips.
3. Five times.
4. Round the edges, on the top, round the bottom, lick the sides.
5. 'Stick' and 'quick'.
6. Answer stating that if the sun shines the lolly is more likely to melt more quickly.
7. Answer stating other things that need to be eaten quickly in the sun, like ice cream!
8. Child's own poem of something else that is messy to eat, e.g. spaghetti, an ice cream, candy floss.

RESOURCE SHEET ANSWERS

Support

1. 'Lick' is written five times in the poem.
2. The poem states you need to lick the lolly round the edges, on the top, round the bottom, on the sides.
3. 'Stick' and 'quick' rhyme with 'lick'.

Extension

Individual responses.

GOING DEEPER

- Review the children's answers to the questions. Children explain which poem they prefer and why. They can discuss what they like and don't like about the poems.
- Share the children's poem about messy food. Make a class poetry book.
- Find other poems the children may like about food.

Key Stage 1 Example Test Paper Answers

CONTENT DOMAINS

1a	1b	1c	1d	1e
Draw on knowledge of vocabulary to understand texts.	Identify and explain key aspects of fiction and non-fiction texts, such as characters, events, titles and information.	Identify and explain the sequence of events in texts.	Make inferences from the text.	Predict what might happen on the basis of what has been read so far.

PAPER 1

The First Flying Machines

Qu	Domain	Answers	Mark	Comment
1	1b	the bat	1	
2	1a	biplane	1	
3	1b	1896	1	
4	1d	Answer that suggests Otto was an inventor who tried to design flying machines that could glide.	1	
5	1b	bicycles	1	
6	1b	Answer that suggests the Wright brothers really wanted to fly.	1	
7	1b	Answer that suggests that unlike a glider the Flyer had an engine and two propellers.	1	
8	1b	Orville Wright	1	
9	1d	Answer that makes reference to the stamp picturing the Wright brothers.	1	

Frog is Fast

10	1b	Rabbit	1	
11	1b	Answer that suggests that Rabbit was someone new to race and someone new to beat.	1	
12	1a	zippy	1	
13	1d	Answer that suggests Rabbit might be surprised because he had only just met Frog or because he was a good runner and knew he would beat Frog.	1	
14	1b	the old tree	1	
15	1b	Rabbit	1	
16	1a	Cross	1	
17	1a	win against	1	
18	1b	Answer that suggests Frog's idea was to race on a bike.	1	
19	1d	Answer that suggests that Rabbit was at a disadvantage because he didn't have a bike.	1	
20	1d	Answer that suggests he was pleased, did a dance and sang a song.	1	
TOTAL			20	

PAPER 2
Trouble in the Rockies

Qu	Domain	Answers	Mark	Comment
1	1b	their next campsite	1	
2	1b	'Will we be safe?'	1	
3	1d	Answer that suggests Eric will keep them safe.	1	
4	1b	two	1	
5	1a	at risk of becoming extinct	1	
6	1b	Answer that suggests that they got off their bikes to look at some bears.	1	
7	1b	Any two of the following: tumbled slid swept fell down	1	
8	1d	Answer that suggests Tom was shocked and frightened.	1	
9	1c	3 Mum held on to Tom's hand. 4 Tom's feet touched the bottom of the river. 1 Mum and Tom found themselves in the river. 2 Tom couldn't find Mum.	1	
10	1d	Answer that suggests they could: 1 keep holding on to the rock, but would be in danger of being attacked by the bears. 2 let go of the rock and get away from the bears but risk being drowned in the river.	2	Award **one** mark for mentioning the danger of getting out of the river and **one** mark for mentioning the danger of staying in it.
11	1d	Answer that suggests that the helmets have protected their heads during their fall in the landslide.	1	
12	1b	Answer that highlights 'In the fading light' suggesting it is now early evening	1	

The Great Blast – Location: the nose

13	1b	waterproofs	1	
14	1b	Any three of the following: dark damp windy hairy sticky warm	1	
15	1b	The hairs in the nose: 1 warm the air. 2 filter the air.	1	
16	1a	detect	1	
17	1b	Answer that suggest the particles from the hot chocolate enter the nose where the millions of nerve cells sense them sending a message to the brain telling the person to enjoy the hot chocolate.	2	Award **one** mark for mentioning particles and nerve cells and **two** marks for including a message being sent to the brain
18	1d, 1e	a sneeze could blow you out of the nose	1	
TOTAL			20	